The Journey: Truths of Same-Gender-Loving Black Males in Higher Education

EMERALD: RESEARCH, THEORY, AND PRACTICE WITHIN ACADEMIC AFFAIRS

SERIES EDITORS:
Antione D. Tomlin, Anne Arundel Community College
Sherella Cupid, Louisiana State University

Series Description

The mission of the Research, Theory, and Practice Within Academic Affairs seeks to explore current trends, practices, and challenges within academic affairs.

This book series will include a plethora of topics with particular attention to the personal and live experiences of individuals who work in higher education academic affairs spaces in various colleges and universities. The intended audience is academic affairs administrators, leaders, educators, policymakers, researchers, and others interested in learning more about the experiences of academic affairs professionals.

Recently Published Titles

When We Hear Them: Attuning Teachers to Language-Diverse Learners (2024)
    Owen Silverman Andrews, & Antione D. Tomlin

The Handbook for Aspiring Higher Education Leaders (2024)
    Antione D. Tomlin

Effective Alternative Assessment Practices in Higher Education (2024)
    Antione D. Tomlin & Christine M. Nowik

Voices of the Field: DEIA Champions in Higher Education (2023)
    Antione D. Tomlin & Sherella Cupid

Black Faculty Do It All: A Moment in The Life of a Blackademic (2023)
    Antione D. Tomlin

Don't Forget About the Adjuncts! (2023) Antione D. Tomlin

The Journey: Truths of Same-Gender-Loving Black Males in Higher Education

EDITED BY

ANTIONE D. TOMLIN

Anne Arundel Community College

emerald
PUBLISHING

United Kingdom – North America – Japan – India – Malaysia – China

Emerald Publishing Limited
Emerald Publishing, Floor 5, Northspring, 21-23 Wellington Street, Leeds LS1 4DL

First edition 2025

Published under exclusive licence by Emerald Publishing Limited.
Reprints and permissions service

Contact: www.copyright.com

British Library Cataloguing in Publication Data

A catalogue record for this book is available from the British Library

ISBNs:
978-1-83708-498-2 HB
978-1-83708-499-9 PB
978-1-83708-500-2 EPDF
978-1-83708-501-9 EPUB

CONTENTS

INTRODUCTION

A RARE SPACE TO COMMUNICATE, SHARE, AND EMBRACE BLACK, SAME GENDER-LOVING, MALE EXPERIENCES

Antione D. Tomlin

This text stands apart from others, and so does its introduction. The motivation behind this work is to provide a platform for Black same-gender-loving (SGL) men in higher education to articulate their experiences in a space that, while making recent strides toward inclusivity, has historically been exclusive. Each narrative within these pages opens a window for authors to share their journey—capturing moments of resilience, invaluable lessons, and the navigation of obstacles to stand proudly in their Black brilliance. Focused on the narratives of Black male SGL students, faculty, and staff in higher education, this text encapsulates the essence of what it means to be a Black male and SGL in the academic realm. As a Black gay male, this project holds personal significance for me, providing a rare space to openly communicate, share, and embrace Black, gay, male experiences within

The Journey: Truths of Same-Gender-Loving Black Males in Higher Education, pages vii–xvi.
Copyright © 2025 *Antione D. Tomlin*
Published under exclusive licence by Emerald Publishing Limited
ISBNs: 978-1-83708-498-2 HB, 978-1-83708-499-9 PB,
978-1-83708-500-2 EPDF, 978-1-83708-501-9 EPUB

higher education. Each section unfolds as an individual narrative, emphasizing the importance of every unique story.

NARRATIVE ONE: QUARENESS EMBODIED: LIVING AUTHENTICALLY AT THE INTERSECTIONS OF SEXUALITY, RACE, PROFESSIONALISM AND ABILITY

In this captivating narrative, Andre' Ford delves into the intricate tapestry of his Black male life, navigating the complex intersections of race, gender, sexuality, and ability within the realm of higher education. The story unfolds against the backdrop of the Southern United States, where Andre's upbringing is intricately woven with the threads of religion, shaping the very fabric of his identity. As we journey through the narrative, Andre' artfully unravels the impact of minority stress, drawing from Meyer's seminal work in 2003, and highlights the indispensable nature of resilience for triumph in his professional pursuits. Echoes of the subject's evolution resonate through recollections of his odyssey towards self-acceptance, interwoven with experiences working with LGBTQIA+ youth and students. The narrative gains depth as Andre' reconciles not only with his queer identity but also grapples with the nuances of disability. In his quest to be a beacon of inspiration, he strives to carve a path where a queer-identified Black man can flourish in academia, seamlessly blending teaching, research, and service. Amidst the journey towards self-discovery, Andre' explores the delicate dance of developing an integrated identity, seeking equilibrium between the personal and professional realms, all the while navigating the undercurrents of heteronormativity. The narrative continues to develop from a lens and approach of quare theory, as elucidated by Johnson in 2001, manifesting within the academic landscape. In a powerful demonstration of "theories in the flesh," the narratives weave real-life examples, dissecting individual and collective identities. The aim is to unravel the challenges and opportunities that arise at the crossroads of research and practice. The spotlight then shifts to the collaborative efforts of a queer-identified Black male professional, working hand-in-hand with BIPOC LGBTQIA+ students. Andre' notes, together, they strive to create spaces that not only affirm identities but also foster inclusivity and learning. Andre's narrative invites readers into a rich space of sharing, where personal stories, academic theories, and societal challenges converge. It serves as a testament to the resilience, determination, and transformative power inherent in the journey of a Black man at the crossroads of identity, academia, and advocacy.

NARRATIVE TWO: OBSCURITY OF BLACK GAY MALES IN ACADEMIC WORKPLACES

Embarking on the academic journey, Dr. Kelly Wallace emphasizes that one is quick to notice the deeply entrenched roots in heterosexual identities. The pervasive influence of white culture casts an imposing shadow, erecting formidable barriers for people of color attempting not only to exist in these scholarly spaces but also to navigate them authentically. Within this landscape, the unique intersection of being Black and Gay often remains unacknowledged or, worse, entirely disregarded. In the hallowed halls of academia, where colleagues predominantly do not share these dual identities and lived experiences, the plight of Black Gay men unfolds. Isolation and roadblocks become familiar companions in their educational odyssey. The absence of supportive systems compounds the challenge, leaving scant resources for cultivating a healthy work/life balance. This narrative is more than an exploration; it is a narrative voyage through Dr. Wallace's experiences as a Black Gay male educator. Through the lens of his personal story, he unveils the triumphs and tribulations that have dotted his path in academia. It's a tale of resilience, a testament to the fortitude required to navigate a system where one's identity often stands at odds with the established norms. Amidst the narrative, successes emerge as beacons of hope, proving that despite the prevailing challenges, strides can be made. Yet, the journey is far from smooth, and the challenges are not mere footnotes; they are integral spaces shaping the narrative. Each obstacle becomes a stepping stone, paving the way for recommendations aimed at fortifying an inclusive work environment for Black Gay men. This narrative is not just a reflection but a call to action. It beckons academia to acknowledge, embrace, and uplift the voices and experiences of Black Gay educators. It serves as a blueprint for fostering an environment where diversity is not merely acknowledged but celebrated, where the richness of identity is seen as an asset rather than an anomaly. In sharing his story, Dr. Wallace aims to contribute to the ongoing dialogue surrounding inclusivity, urging academia to evolve into a space where every voice, irrespective of its intersectionality, resonates and thrives.

NARRATIVE THREE: IT WASN'T JUST A PHASE

In the backdrop of societal expectations dictating that a man should be with a woman, and vice versa, Desmond Dunklin shares how his emotions defied the conventional narrative. Desmond explores a past experience: He, a figure of strength and inked artistry, lived just across the college hall, standing at 5'10, weighing 175 lbs. Our connection ran deeper than the surface, transcending the boundaries set by societal norms. We shared more than just space; we shared workouts, study sessions, and the narratives of our most profound traumas. In him, I found a sanctuary—a place where he felt secure. Our bond was rooted in genuine friendship and love, unburdened by the constraints of societal expectations. Little did I know that one evening would alter the course of our connection forever. As we sipped drinks and immersed ourselves in a movie, he broke the silence with unexpected words, "Dez, you know I love you, bro." My reflexive response echoed the camaraderie we had built, "I love you too, bro." However, he rose from his seat, solemnly declaring, "No, Dez, I am in love with you." Shock and amazement coursed through me as he walked over and sealed his confession with a kiss. In that moment, the torrent of emotions, thoughts, and fantasies that had been swirling within me for years crystallized into reality. Someone out there loved me for exactly who I was. They saw my flaws, yet their love endured. It was a revelation, a confirmation that what I felt wasn't a passing phase—it was real, genuine, and profoundly transformative. Love, in its purest form, had entered my life, bringing with it an overwhelming sense of happiness and authenticity. Everything I had been feeling all of these years, the emotions, thoughts, fantasy, it was real. There was somebody out there who loved me for me. Who genuinely loved me and saw all of my flaws, yet they still loved me. I knew then, it wasn't just a phase, It was real. It was love. It was happiness.

NARRATIVE FOUR: DUOETHNOGRAPHY: TRUTH TELLING, DIFFERENCES AND COMMONALITIES IN THE EXPERIENCES OF TWO SAME-GENDER LOVING BLACK MEN IN ACADEMIA

Embark on a riveting duoethnographic expedition as this narrative unfolds, chronicling the intertwined tales of two Black gay men, Dr. Andrew Campbell and Dr. Kaschka Watson, who have traversed the challenging terrain of homophobia in Jamaica, only to find themselves as educational leaders in Canada. Their narrative journey is not merely an exploration of similarities, differences, and nuances but a deep dive into the emotional tapestry of their experiences. Through the lens of duoethnographic methodology, Dr. Campbell and Dr. Watson wove personal reflective narratives, each strand pulsating with raw emotions. Rooted in reflective research, this approach became the vessel through which they dissected their encounters with homophobia, scrutinizing the intersections of their identities. The stories they share transcend mere recounting; they stand as empowering narratives poised to disrupt and dismantle the pervasive homophobia in the Caribbean. Dr. Campbell and Dr. Watson's collaboration unfolded over five virtual encounters, facilitated by the digital realm of Zoom, where they delved into four core topics central to our experiences as gay men. The conversations, meticulously audio-recorded, captured not just the words exchanged but the nuances of their emotions, gestures, and expressions—a rich tapestry of their shared narratives. These recordings, both verbal and non-verbal, encapsulated the essence of their lived experiences. In the ebb and flow of their dialogues, they found themselves traversing uncharted territories—core topics emerging organically, unscripted. Recognizing these serendipitous detours, they navigated back to the heart of their discussions. Post each meeting, a meticulous review of their shared narratives enriched the depth of their data collection and analysis. As educational leaders within the Canadian academy, their reflections unveil the tensions and traumas of their time as gay men in a homophobic Jamaican landscape. Yet, within the folds of adversity, they spotlight their navigation of those experiences, emerging not only as successful gay scholars but also as impassioned activists for the LGBTQ+ community. Their journey transcends borders, weaving a narrative that intertwines personal resilience, academic prowess, and advocacy in a symphony of triumph over adversity.

NARRATIVE FIVE: AM I BLACK AND GAY ENOUGH?

Dr. Richard Marks, Jr. invites us to step into the intricate dance of identity, where the celebration of being Black and gay echoes louder than ever before. In this evolving narrative, intersectionality emerges as the unapologetic vehicle that traverses the landscapes of race, gender, sexual orientation, and myriad identities. Yet, society, with its penchant for simplicity, often insists on the singularity of identity, pressuring individuals to choose one facet to define their essence. Within the experiences of the Black community, a dichotomy persists, wherein LGBTQIA individuals find themselves subjected to ostracization and shame, birthing a tumultuous mix of confusion, anger, and racial-cultural dissonance (Marks, 2015). As society propels the notion of embracing multiple identities, the internal struggle becomes palpable. For Dr. Marks, a Black gay male administrator navigating the corridors of higher education, the question arises—which identity takes precedence, gay or Black? This narrative is a canvas painted with the hues of his experiences as a Black, gay higher education administrator. However, it is a mere glimpse into a realm where much more exploration is warranted. The spotlight, historically fixated on the experiences of Black gay students, now beckons toward the often-neglected narratives of Black gay faculty and staff within the educational context. In the vast landscape of academia, the research on the experiences of Black gay faculty and staff is a glaring void. It is not merely limited; it is virtually non-existent. This narrative serves as a call to arms, a plea for the amplification of voices that remain obscured. To understand the success and challenges woven into the journeys of Black gay faculty and staff navigating the complex culture of higher education administration, research is not just desirable; it is imperative. As administrators, Dr. Marks emphasized that voices hold the power to shape the narrative, not only for himself but for the students we strive to guide. The call for research is a call for advocacy, a declaration that stories of Black, gay, men matter, and experiences are integral to the fabric of higher education. In the absence of Black, gay, male voices, we risk failing not only ourselves but the very students we are entrusted to support and uplift. The time is now to raise the voices of Black, gay, male administrators, to be heard, and to pave the way for a more inclusive and empathetic educational landscape.

NARRATIVE SIX: HEY CIS!

In this narrative journey, Sean Rice, Jr. delves into the transformative power of understanding intersectionality and allyship, as he navigates the intricate terrain of living unapologetically in both his queerness and Blackness within the realm of higher education—a journey that seamlessly evolved into his chosen profession. In the symphony of advice echoing from elders, young Black men are urged to walk with heads held high. Yet, the question lingers: who guides the gaze of Black queer individuals, navigating a world that often dehumanizes them based on their sexuality? This narrative unveils the story of how, against the backdrop of societal expectations, Sean's personal evolution unfolded, shaped by his rela- tionships with cis heterosexuals and those actively committed to allyship. The crux lies in the term "active"—an ally, not a mere noun but a verb, embodying a continuous commitment to understanding and supporting the multifaceted nature of my identity. The narrative unfolds as he dissects pivotal moments where these relationships empowered him to cultivate self-awareness and authorship over his own experience. Friendship emerges as a crucial theme, an avenue through which bonds are formed, understanding is cultivated, and support becomes a tangible force. The significance of developing connections with others, especially those who stand as allies, becomes a cornerstone in his journey. Yet, the most pivotal relationship explored is the one with the "man in the mirror"—an introspective exploration that laid the foundation for embracing the entirety of Sean's identity. This chapter is not just a reflection on personal experiences; it is a testament to the power of active allyship and the evolution that unfolds when genuine connections are forged. It speaks to the transformative potential of relationships in navigat- ing the complexities of identity. As the narrative unfolds, it beckons readers to reconsider the role of allyship, not as a passive concept but as a dynamic force that, when harnessed, can guide individuals towards authentic self-discovery and acceptance.

NARRATIVE SEVEN: IN AUTHENTICITY: (DE)VALUING SAME- GENDER-LOVING "BLAQUEER" MEN IN HIGHER EDUCATION

In Dr. David Sterling Brown's narrative, he builds upon Dr. T Anansi Wilson's groundbreaking concept of "BlaQueer," a recognition of the dual identity of being openly Black and queer. This narrative unfolds as a challenge to the ivory towers of higher education, urging institutions to confront the perilous oversight of neglect- ing the protection of the vulnerable Black and queer population. Dr. Brown direct- ly confronts the paradoxes inherent in Diversity, Equity, and Inclusion (DEI) and anti-racist agendas that, despite their noble intentions, can inadvertently perpetu- ate anti-Black and homophobic practices. As the narrative unfurls, the rewards of embracing a BlaQueer positionality in higher education are acknowledged, cast- ing light on the resilience that arises from navigating this unique intersection. Woven into the fabric of his narrative are the threads of personal-experiential an- ecdotes, carefully disclosed. These narratives serve as critical engagements with the pervasive issue of sexual violence, providing a lens through which the reader can intimately connect with the challenges faced by the BlaQueer community within the academic landscape. A discerning critique surfaces as Dr. Brown ex- amines the prevalent usage of "safe space" rhetoric within higher education. The narrative contends that, rather than seeking an illusory safety, institutions should embrace and advocate for a "productive discomfort" philosophy. This philosophy recognizes the inherent impossibility of everyone attaining or feeling absolute safety in any given moment, challenging the traditional narrative surrounding safe spaces. Additionally, this narrative, with its immersive exploration of BlaQueer experiences, not only challenges the status quo but also serves as a call to action for higher education institutions. It beckons them to reevaluate their practices, fostering an environment where the vulnerable Black and queer population can thrive, unencumbered by the shadows of systemic biases.

NARRATIVE EIGHT: BARELY GETTING BI

Eric Martin shares a personal narrative that unfolds within the unique landscape of historically Black colleges and universities (HBCUs) in the United States. This narrative is a journey through uncharted territory, where Eric assumed the pioneering role of leading the first LGBTQ center in the southeast region. An additional layer to this groundbreaking venture was being the inaugural Black cis-male to serve as the coordinator of the center. Anticipating the challenges that accompanied this role, he willingly stepped into uncharted waters. However, what Eric wasn't prepared for was the profound impact this position would have on his own intersecting identities, adding intricate layers to his personal narrative. Amid the timeless battle of navigating the complexities of Black identity, a new challenge emerged—the subtle yet palpable waves of bi-erasure within this predominantly Black space. Choosing this professional journey meant embracing the assumption that he would be perceived as gay, a label he readily accepted given the nature of the work, particularly in higher education. However, the real challenge lay in the scarcity of bisexual representation in this field, exacerbating the complexities of his own assimilation. This narrative delves into the nuanced journey of unpacking this assimilation, unveiling its close relationship to the broader assimilation that many Black men undertake in their quest for acceptance within the confines of masculinity. As the narrative unfolds, it traverses the unexplored landscapes of identity, representation, and the intricate dance between personal authenticity and societal expectations. This is not just a story; it is a personal odyssey through uncharted territories, a testament to the transformative power of embracing one's identity, even when the path is laden with challenges and uncharted complexities.

ALL EXPERIENCES MATTER

In addition to asking all of the men to write about their narratives and sharing the stories that needed to be heard, I also asked them to briefly share an experience that helped shape their identity as a Black, same-gender-loving male. Take a look at some of the experiences below:

> An experience that I had as a same gender loving Black male within the field of higher education, was when I participated as a part of an oral history project exploring my reasons for relocating from the South to New York City. My rationale at the time was that I needed a space to explore my sexuality and identity that wasn't under the gaze of my religious upbringing. As a young adult I learned that my sexuality was to remain private and secretive and that to acknowledge my queerness within a professional setting was not only unnecessary but ill advised. However, as I started

my work in the nonprofit sector and worked with young adults who were out, I began to develop the courage to become transparent about my identity. When I transitioned to a community college, I began to embrace it not as an ally to LGBTQIA+ students, but also as a burgeoning content expert on issues affecting my community by facilitating cultural competency trainings and workshops. As a doctoral student at the University of Alabama, I advocate for authentic inclusion of LGBTQIA+ students through my research and service to the college. Participating in this oral history project gave me the opportunity to curate my journey and to publicly celebrate myself as a pansexual Black man thriving in the academic space.

—Andre' Ford

Being socialized in a world where Black and same-gender loving men didn't exist was the biggest challenge for me in developing into the person and professional I am today. For example, growing up in a family where everyone is heterosexual. Or watching television where there were very few shows that presented both Black and same-gender loving relationships in a positive light. These moments shaped an early belief that being a Black and same-gender loving male are not identities that society would happily embrace. Additionally, these stereotypes and false narratives contributed to my internalization of not being able to be successful. This birthed imposter syndrome. However, the top three pivotal moments where this shifted for me were in college, graduate school, and getting my doctorate degree. Yes, academia was my pathway to not only prove myself but break barriers that existed in the world. In most of the academic and similar spaces I have been in, I have been the only self-identified same-gender loving person. This dominance of heterosexual identities further pushed me to make my presence known and do work to increase visibility of my communities and be a leader for the next generation of Black and Gay men.

—Dr. Kelly Wallace

As a man of color, our image and reputation is everything. I have always kept my personal life and my private life separately. However, when I transitioned into higher education, I saw men who walked like me, talked like me, but also lived their truth in secret like me. It wasn't until I attended a higher education conference where I met this amazing Black man and he told me these words. No matter what you do in this life to thy own self always be true. You have one life, so live it and live it unapologetically. From that moment on, I begin to live my truth. One thing that I have learned is that people will not always respect your choices of how you live your life, however they will respect how you carry yourself when you live the life that you live in a positive light. So today, I am living my life mentoring, coaching, and inspiring the next generation of same gender-living males, because you only have one life to live and you can have it all. Success, love, truth, respect, but most importantly a life free from shame and guilt of denying who you are.

—Desmond Dunklin

As an undergrad in the early 90s, the phenomenon around Black gayness centered around the "DL Brutha" and "Don't ask, don't tell" campaigns. I navigated the world of the "DL Brutha" quite well. I dated men and women, taking on the conquest typical of the hyper-sexual Black male stereotype. College was a space and place for self-discovery. In many ways, I took full advantage. Matriculating in my academics while growing more aware of my sexual preference and comfort in accepting who I was, I began reading books to help me understand my feelings and how I lived. I was dating women to please others, but behind closed doors, secretly in the desire to spend my time with the same gender. While learning more about gayness, it often felt like I had to choose between the two. It was not until I learned about intersectionality that I proudly embraced them both.

—*Dr. Richard Marks, Jr.*

One experience that helped shape my identity as a Black, same-gender-loving male was during the height of the pandemic and quarantining. At that time, everyone was stuck inside, while also seeking community outside of our own minds. I was able to find community and curate a space on the audio app, "Clubhouse". I came together with a group of talented Black Queer men to create the group, "Black Gay Men Chat"! On the app, we were able to educate and highlight the lived experiences of Black SGL men across the world. I tapped into my creativity and my voice in so many ways, by producing multiple projects such as: a talent show through the "Black & Gay" group, a seductive improv audio show, "The Art of Seduction", a shoot your shot show "The Black Gay Bachelor", a book club called "Reading Rainbow", and facilitating/moderating multiple conversations across the platform (crystal meth in the Black Queer community, Black Gay Fatherhood, Dating Red Flags, etc.). This experience shaped my identity because I was able to share/facilitate a space with individuals that were able to challenge me and validate my lived experiences, while bringing new perspectives to the conversations. Our group currently has 7,000+ members and showed me the power and influence that we have as Black Queer people when we come together. I recognize that at times society will not accept us fully which was evident in heterosexual spaces on the app where the expectation was for us to show-up "Black first", but we are full people, and we deserve to share and take up all the space we desire, while standing in all that we are. This experience was empowering, inspiring, and made me feel seen holistically.

—*Sean Rice, Jr.*

Serving as the first Black male coordinator of a LGBTQ center on a HBCU campus has without a doubt shaped my experience as a SGL cis-male completely. Entering this role has been a blessing that's allowed me to have an impact on a community that I care so deeply about but also continues to illustrate a disconnect between two of my salient intersecting identities. On a campus where my center exists mere feet away from the Men's Center, I've experienced students and staff who avoided eye contact with me, barely engaged in our "collaborations", and chose to only talk from the doorway of the center instead of coming in. But in accepting this role, it also meant accepting all the razzle dazzle that came with it, including the looks of shock I get when people hear my official job title and watching other men tense up in casual conversation. My experience with maleness in tandem with my own sexual orientation and profession are something that I find to always be in question by other people, men specifically. And it fuels the fire and desire that I have to do my part in dismantling the oppressive nature that keeps men away from the understanding that true DEI work is not just the advancement of cishet men, but for all of us.

—*Eric D. Martin*

With this introduction, we pivot to the narratives and vignettes that amplify the diverse voices of same-gender-loving, Black men. To Andre', Aaron, Kelly, Anthony, Desmond, Andrew, Kaschka, Brandon, Richard, Sean, Rodrick, David, D, and Eric thank you! Without y'all this project would not be possible. I am extremely proud of you all and excited for what is next! Again, thank you, much peace and love.

—Antione D. Tomlin, Ph.D.

QUARENESS EMBODIED

Living Authentically at the Intersections of Sexuality, Race, Professionalism and Ability

Andre Ford

La Guardia Community College

This chapter explores the impacts of a Black man living at the intersections of race, gender, sexuality, and ability within a higher education setting. By examining the subject's upbringing in the Southern United States and the role religion played in his identity formation, the author seeks to explore the cumulative effects of minority stress (Meyer, 2003) and the essentialness of developing resilience to succeed in his profession. This chapter will include recollections of the subject's journey to self-acceptance through work with lesbian, gay, bisexual, transgender, queer/questioning, intersex, asexual and other sexual and gender identities (LGBTQIA+) youth and students, while reconciling his own identity because of a disability and the desire to serve as a role model of how a queer identified Black man can thrive in the academy through teaching, research, and service. The author will explore the concept of developing an integrated identity in which achieving a homeostasis between the personal and professional is discussed within and in tension with heteronormativity. The goal is to identify ways in which quare theory (Johnson, 2001) manifests within academia. By providing real life examples of "theories in the flesh" (Johnson,

The Journey: Truths of Same-Gender-Loving Black Males in Higher Education, pages 1–12.
Copyright © 2025 *Antione D. Tomlin*
Published under exclusive licence by Emerald Publishing Limited
ISBNs: 978-1-83708-498-2 HB, 978-1-83708-499-9 PB,
978-1-83708-500-2 EPDF, 978-1-83708-501-9 EPUB

2001), in which individual and collective identity is investigated, the author intends to explore the challenges and opportunities of working at the intersection of research and practice. Furthermore, this chapter will explore the salient issues that arise as a queer identified Black male professional works in collaboration with BIPOC (Black, Indigenous, and People of Color) LGBTQIA+ students in creating identity affirming and inclusive learning spaces.

Keywords: Minority Stress, Quare Theory; Personal and Professional Identity

INTRODUCTION

Within the field of higher education most studies concur that lack of representation of Black men effects environments on campus, retention of students, and the accessibility of role models who are Black males (Harper & Simmons, 2018; Henry, 2021). As an adult and continuing education instructor and program manager who has experience in both non-profit and higher education, I am acutely aware of the importance of representation and the essentialness of students identifying with educators who look like them. This is more apparent because I am a Black male, pansexual, white-collar professional, who possesses an advanced degree. As a social worker, I am ethically obligated to practice cultural humility, with the objective of dismantling racist and oppressive systems (National Association of Social Workers, 2021). Community colleges have served as an access point to a better quality of life for several groups who have traditionally experienced marginalization and oppression. These institutions are potentially capable of uplifting the socio-economic status of members of the LGBT community, especially those who have experienced disproportionate higher rates of poverty, including bisexual and transgender people, as compared to heterosexual and cis-gender individuals (Badgett et al., 2019; Conron et al., 2022). While being mindful of my individual journey, I must be unyielding in my quest for equality which calls for ameliorating of injustices that are systematically and structurally embedded (Bernstein et al., 2020), all while in pursuit of social justice, for the population I am called to serve and to whom I also identify with.

My name is Andre J. Ford. I was born in Houston, Texas at the dawn of the Reagan Revolution. I grew up in a working-class community in which both of my parents worked at their respective jobs until retirement. We were not rich and despite their divorce, I never went without, and I was fortunate that my father was a constant and consistent presence in my life. This was also a time in which I would encounter role models who either passed away due to complications of acquired immunodeficiency syndrome (AIDS) or who managed to survive the initial onslaught of the epidemic. The outcome was usually delineated along lines of race, economic status and class, in which young Black men were its causalities. As I bore witness to this, I realized the potential risks and pitfalls of being a same gender loving Black man. This would profoundly shape my personal life, as well as my career trajectory. My journey to living authentically would require a change in my basic assumptions about how I would choose to show up in professional settings. As a burgeoning practitioner scholar and social activist, my life experiences have shaped me into the pragmatic individual that I am today. This chapter will explore major events in my life and how they informed my experience as a same gender loving Black man who is thriving in the community college space.

GROWING UP AS A QUEER BLACK BOY IN THE SOUTH

I am the youngest of three boys. As a child I was introverted and shy, until my mother allowed me to participate in the Easter program at the Christian primary school that I attended. It was here that I learned the importance of decorum, following every question or call of my name with a *yes or no mam or a yes or no sir*, in deference to my parents or any adult who occupied the room. As a child I would recite such classics as *The Creation* and *The Prodigal Son,* both by James Weldon Johnson, to the approval and applause of my congregation. It was here where I would find my voice, only to have it silenced for fear of going to hell. This experience was traumatic. I would literally attempt to block out invasive thoughts in my mind as I developed an intense crush on an older boy at the age of 15. I navigated this by telling myself that as long as I didn't act on my desires, that I would remain in God's will. I became an expert at impulse control, almost to the point of being obsessive compulsive. I didn't allow myself to experiment with my sexuality. It was something that was to remain unexplored until adulthood. I came of age during the media sanctioned "downlow phenomenon," which described some Black men as out, however, the majority of them were secretly having sex with other men and as a result adhered to the expectations of parenthood and masculinity while associating homosexuality primarily with Whiteness (Denizet-Lewis, 2003). This allowed the human immunodeficiency virus (HIV) and AIDS to become pervasive in the African American community, with gay and bisexual Black men being reduced to incubators and disease spreaders. The message was clear for me as an adolescent who was starting to experience same sex attraction. That my feelings were wrong, unnatural, and abominable in the sight of God. I would find refuge in the words of Ntozake Shange and Zora Neale Hurston, who both pleaded for the liberation of women within their works. I too wanted to be loved and to be warmly embraced (Shange, 1975). I valiantly attempted to remain faithful to my Southern Baptist up binging by briefly participating in the now defunct Exodus International, which promised deliverance from homosexuality by virtue of prayer and counseling (Lovett, 2013). I decided to join this group after watching a news segment about it on my local television station. To my recollection the subject of the segment had been "delivered" from homosexuality and was happily married to his wife. The group had a clear hypothesis of the causes of same sex attraction and ways to combat it. Their theory was reasonable in my view. However, after taking part in group sessions where participants who were married with children we still struggling with their desires, something in me internally felt that their conversions weren't true. Therefore, I decided to leave the group. It was then that I, as so many same-gender loving Black men before me had done, would "move up North" to re-discover who I was. Individuals who relocate to places outside the South such as New York City and other urban settings are better equipped to manage sexual marginalization over their lifetimes (Scott, 2021). My life in the South was one that revolved around God, family and the intense love and commitment that I gave to both. This prepared me for the next stage of my life, as my identity evolved. The following section will provide examples of how I began to successfully integrate my personal and professional identity, eventually becoming a content expert on issues concerning BIPOC LGBTQIA+ students in higher education, a role model for what it means to be a queer Black man pursuing doctoral education and the strategies and recommendations that I would share with others like me who are currently navigating academia.

INTEGRATING MY PERSONAL AND PROFESSIONAL IDENTITY

The state of mental health for the LGBTQIA+ community is challenging with disproportionate negative outcomes for a POC. When compared to the larger community, individuals who are LGBTQ POC, experience mental health challenges at higher levels (Human Rights Campaign, 2021b). This and other issues which were evident before the Co-Vid pandemic, have prompted higher education and other service-oriented institutions to intentionally promote diversity, equity, and inclusion, even though evidence is emerging of retrenchment from those efforts across multiple industries. Furthermore, it is essential to explore how BIPOC LGBTQIA+ employees effectively utilize their personal and professional identity to combat the inherent racism and oppression that exists in institutions. It is only by advocating for the implementation of specific policies that create an inclusive organizational climate and culture(Schneider et al., 2013), while also modeling these behaviors that will lead to impactful change. This section will explore some of the challenges that I experienced as a same gender loving Black men in academia. We will also explore how my professional identity was impacted by working with BIPOC LGBTQIA+ youth, how I became a model employee, and intentionally chose to take a proactive role in bridging the gap between practice and research, in which I partner with BIPOC LGBTQIA+ faculty, students and staff in sharing their knowledge and wisdom in what it takes to create a truly diverse, equitable and inclusive campus environment.

Witnessing Resilience

I started teaching adult and continuing education students in my mid-twenties. I worked as an instructor at a shelter that assisted youth with transitioning from homelessness to stable housing, most of whom were BIPOC. Several of them were also LGBTQIA+ and had to contend with multiple stressors at the intersections of race, ethnicity, sexual orientation, gender identity and expression. LGBT youth experience homelessness or instability at a rate of 28%, with higher rates being reported by transgender/non-binary youth (The Trevor Project, 2022.) As I worked with these students, I was humbled by their resilience, bravery, and courage in the face of daunting odds. They encouraged me to collaborate with them to create a learning environment that was trauma informed and culturally responsive. As I pursued my Master of Social Work degree, I was able to synthesize my newfound knowledge, with my understanding of pedagogy, curriculum development, and instruction, to promote diversity, equity, and inclusion(DEI) within my classroom. This was fundamentally important for all the students, but particularly for those who were LGBTQIA+ as I formed relationships with them. LGBT youth who develop connections can diminish the effects of stressors which helps alleviate minority stress and the mental health issues associated with it (Meyer, 2003; Robinson, 2021). I did this while being mindful of the importance of maintaining professional boundaries. I also came from a background in which I was taught that my personal life was to remain private. Therefore, I consistently negotiated within myself of whether if or when it was appropriate to disclose my sexual orientation. The guiding principle being, if it was of service to the student in seeing someone "like them", so they could know that achieving their goals was possible.

Model Employee

Higher education has grappled with diversity in leadership and faculty roles at higher education institutions (Gasman et al., 2015; Henry, 2021). I experienced this as I transitioned from working in the non-profit sector to a community college in the adult and continuing education division. Even though I was an educator and program supervisor, I was not classified as faculty. The title was reserved for those who taught credit-bearing courses. Most professional development opportunities were designed for them. This put me at a disadvantage because the learning needs of my students were not necessarily the same as those who were pursuing a college degree. I once again felt "othered" as I did during other critical junctures in my personal and professional life. I assumed ultimate responsibility for my professional development. This was important as I continued my work with a student population whose unique needs are often overlooked or poorly researched. Furthermore, I worked in a program that served young fathers who were mostly people of color, which caused me to adopt a more masculine demeanor, as to not be outed. My primary concern was whether disclosure of my sexual orientation would have a negative effect on their ability to learn. Therefore, I made the decision to focus on being technically competent in my work and to have above average job performance. I developed culturally responsive curriculum, set up policies and procedures for holistic student evaluation and developed skills in collecting quantitative and qualitative data. My transparency and vulnerability were limited to anecdotes about the loss of my brother to gun violence. I engrossed myself in my work as based upon what I thought a model employee should be. There were no vocal LGBTQIA+ colleagues who could serve as mentors, so I was responsible for navigating this new terrain alone. The purpose of higher education is ascribed to three interconnected missions which include, educating the population, discovering new knowledge and engagement with the community or society at large (Papadimitriou, 2020). It is taken for granted that post-secondary institutions are leaders and innovators in promoting DEI and that there are institutional mechanisms in place to achieve these goals. The journey for me, as it is for so many others, was how to develop an identity that integrates my education, professional background, practice wisdom and the appropriate use of self, to further the mission of the institution in which I am privileged to work. Not having a mentor made me feel uncertain as to my future. There wasn't a model of how to be transparent and open about one's sexual orientation and whether there were unintended consequences by doing so. If I came across as effeminate, would that negatively impact my career? How would I deal with homophobic slurs directed towards me in the classroom if they occurred? There wasn't a guide for me to follow. This caused me to practice hypervigilance in a quest to maintain my personal and professional integrity. However, there are consequences when one can not be their complete authentic self in the workplace.

Identities Converge

The seeds of change were planted at my previous job as I began to become a content expert on issues affecting LGBTQIA+ youth. I would observe that staff members did not have the requisite knowledge to serve this population. There was a need to assist the organization in developing cultural competence to effectively work with this community. I created workshops which gave employees the opportunity to learn about systemic issues impacting LGBTQIA+ youth, basic terminology to understand variation in gender identity, expression, and sexual orientation, while helping employees devise strategies to better assist them with engaging clients. One specific approach was the integration of mindfulness which requires a singularity of focus without distinction between the several facets of one's practice (Epstein, 1999). The purpose is to look at the individual holistically in which one's mental, physical, and spiritual needs are all interwoven. I would cultivate this practice in my work at the community college as an instructor. Two students would serve as role models for me in my development. One was a Latinx transgender woman, who I worked with at my previous job. She demonstrated resilience and pride in herself, withstanding the discrimination, harassment, and prejudice she endured. The second was an African American man who was open about his sexuality despite being in an environment that was potentially hostile. Due to his honesty and transparency, he earned the respect of his peers. These experiences, in addition to my diagnosis with a neurological condition compelled me to take a more proactive role as "out" same gender loving Black man in academia. It all started with numbness and tingling in my hands and feet which became chronic. This escalated to clinical weakness on my left side and subtle but noticeable differences in my cognition and gait. Based on my symptoms, multiple sclerosis(MS) was a possibility. When not enough clinical evidence wasn't available to make a definitive diagnosis for MS, my neurologist determined that my symptoms were idiopathic. It was at this moment that I realized that I would have to live as a fully integrated human being in which my queer identity, Christian faith and Blackness could peacefully co-exist in all facets of my life. The internalized trauma I endured brought me to this point and it was my responsibility to make a change. My well-being and life depended on it.

ONE STEP CLOSER TO SELF-ACTUALIZATION

Further integration of my professional and personal identity took shape when I posted a rainbow flag on my office door. I neither confirmed nor denied my own sexual orientation at work, but this statement was one of communicating to others that I would provide a safe space for LGBTQIA+ students, as well as a sign of resistance in which I subtlety protested the heteronormative privilege that is deeply embedded within our institutions. I would be asked to participate in an oral history project that would chronicle my journey from the South, to my life as a non-heterosexual Black man living in New York City. It was here that I began to operationalize the challenges and rewards of being a professional who was queer and male, while living in a Black body. The challenges included the burdens of being the only one who openly identified as such, maintaining clear boundaries to protect myself, as to not become an unassuming victim of implicit bias and the hypervigilance that comes with deciphering whether I was safe to be my complete and true self in professional settings. My interview was recorded, transcribed, and stored in the college archives. I joined the LGBTQIA+ Advisory Committee, and I would be featured as a part of an exhibit with other faculty and staff members who were a part of the same community, me being the only Black male to be curated. I facilitated a workshop on Ballroom Culture to the Queer Student Club, to share with them the historical underpinnings that have helped queer and trans people of color create community. I was inspired by the fierceness and pride of the participants. My steps towards integration have been incremental, however, each has led me closer to living fully at the intersections of race, ethnicity, sexuality, and gender.

I would begin to formally bridge the gap between my lived experience, practice wisdom, and research when I decided to pursue a Doctor of Social Work (DSW) degree. I chose this approach because it would allow me to develop expertise in the nexus of research and practice. A DSW possesses superior expertise, with profound knowledge in one chosen subject related to the practice of social work and communicates said knowledge through instruction, presentation, practice, and scholarly endeavors (Hartocollis et al., 2015). In so many ways there was a parallel process to my professional development in choosing to make the experiences of BIPOC LGBTQIA+ students the focus of my research. I began to learn about the theoretical frameworks that would undergird my work, which included creating identity affirming learning environments for BIPOC LGBTQIA+ students, and expanded into understanding the experiences of transwomen of color, who are disproportionately victims of fatal violence(Human Rights Campaign, 2021b). It has been in my pursuit of a doctorate that I realized that clinical skill and technical knowledge is not enough. I am obligated to contribute to the practice knowledge base as it pertains to our community and to serve as a bridge in which I partner with relevant stakeholders by virtue of Community Based Participatory Research, which strives to alleviate health disparities through client centered practice and community directed systematic examination (Colins et al., 2019). Further integrating my roles as human, educator, social worker, and researcher will allow me to achieve this goal.

CLAIMING AND CELEBRATING MY AUTHENTIC SELF WITHIN THE ACADEMY

Implications and Recommendations

To address the experiences of what it means to thrive authentically as a same gender loving Black male in the academy, the following recommendations are proposed and are anchored in facilitating change at the micro, mezzo, and macro levels of practice, while utilizing an anti-racist and anti-oppression lens. The implications include developing strategies to break down barriers and to promote authentic inclusion on behalf of the students we serve and of ourselves as professionals.

First, as academicians and leaders, we must take a proactive role in narrowing the gap between research and practice. Identifying an area of interest as it pertains to LGBTQIA+ issues within higher education and collaborating with underrepresented groups in producing research that centers them is essential. As literature on the experiences of Black LGBT students grows, research on Latinx, Native American and Two-Spirit LGBT pupils remains limited (Duran, 2018). We stand in a unique position as allies to develop a culture of mutual trust so that we can contribute to developing a better understanding of groups who have not been adequately represented in the literature.

Second, we must be visible to demonstrate to colleagues and students alike that we are an essential part of the fabric of the campus community and to be role models for BIPOC LGBTQIA+ students. For those who are educators, making our classrooms inclusive spaces produces better academic outcomes. Students identified their campus environments as affirming when faculty address topics within their classes related to race, sexuality, and gender (Garvey et al., 2019). Furthermore, data has revealed that faculty members who are either allies, or identify as queer, and are supportive of students, within educational settings, while visibly interacting with them informally on campus as participants, are identified as sources of support by those who are LGBT (Linley et al., 2016). Staff members can serve as leaders in creating safe zones in their respective departments by promoting best practices that are culturally responsive. Allied groups are fundamental in facilitating spaces for LGBT faculty and staff to combat against homophobia and transphobia (Lesnick, 2021). Promoting proper use of preferred pronouns and advocating for policies which incorporate sexual and gender diversity at the institutional level are also crucial. Gender neutral restrooms, policies inclusive of gender identity that are non-discriminatory and the opportunity to change one's name on academic records without legal proceedings were deemed most important (Goldberg et al., 2019). Our visibility and advocacy at multiple levels within our institutions is fundamental for change.

Theory Meets Practice

Finally, we must honor and celebrate our individual and collective identity as members of the LGBTQIA+ community. By integrating my understanding of intersectionality, minority stress and quare theory with praxis, my work with BIPOC LGBTQIA+ students has evolved. Quare theory (Johnson, 2001) considers how race, class, gender, and sexuality interact (Ellis, 2023; Means & Jaeger, 2013). It articulates the individual and collective experiences of BIPOC LGBTQ-IA+ people, and how they live and create meaning, as they seek to change oppressive systems from within. It consists of four components (Carmicheal, 2023; Johnson, 2001) for which concrete examples of how each one can be translated into practice within higher education settings will be given. Theories in the flesh, highlights the differences within and amongst people of color in the LGBTQ-IA+ community, while synchronously acknowledging the effects of racism and classism in how the community experiences the world by integrating theory and practice as a mode of political resistance (Johnson, 2001). Safe Zone and allyship trainings must recognize that the LGBTQIA+ community is not monolithic and that individuals who are BIPOC must contend with unique challenges that require different solutions. Providing training opportunities for faculty, staff and administrators in identifying racism, transphobia, and homophobia and helping them devise concrete strategies to combat both issues in their areas of practice is essential. Theory of performance cultivates self-empowerment by developing, acknowledging, and maintaining self-assurance and cultural identity despite being in an environment that fails to acknowledge it (Carmichael, 2023; Johnson, 2001). LGBTQIA+ campus organizations have long served as safe spaces of expression for its members. College administrations and other relevant stakeholders must be proactive in their allyship by sponsoring and participating in events which celebrate the LGBTQIA+ community. Performativity calls for Black people to be aware of their past and present in order to understand what it means to live within a Black body (Carmichael, 2023). Educators should include the historical contributions of the LGBTQIA+ community while highlighting the experiences of BIPOC individuals in their curriculum. Trailblazers such as James Baldwin, Bayard Rustin, Audre Lorde, Marsha P. Johnson, Sylvia Rivera, Essex Hemphill and Marlon Riggs should be studied due to their work in the areas of political and social activism, artistry and performance. Finally, contributions from resistance recognizes that Black people have developed resilience and strategies to survive, as manifested in theories of performance and performativity (Carmichael, 2023; Johnson, 2001). A prominent example of this is the evolution of Ballroom Culture from being a once underground movement to becoming mainstream. Blacks and Latinos created this culture in order to celebrate their diversity at the intersections of sexuality, gender identity and expression, while also acknowledging the stressors associated with class and race. From this came the opportunity for the BIPOC LGBTQIA+ community to create meaning in a society that all too easily condemned them, as based upon the aforementioned attributes, while also sharing their dreams and aspirations by virtue of performance. Relevant stakeholders must serve as reservoirs of support in making the larger campus climate and culture truly inclusive. We must ensure that policies which directly impact the progress and advancement of students, faculty, staff and administrators who are BIPOC and LGBTQIA+ are equitable. Operationalizing the approach to your work, while authentically being who you are is where the capacity for professional success and personal fulfillment exists. All while serving as a role model for the next generation of students and colleagues within the community. Our northern star should be to fiercely advocate for the authentic inclusion of the marginalized for which it can be communicated: "When they possess opportunity, we all do" (Crenshaw, 1989).

CONCLUSION

As someone who embodies multiple identities, I am mindful of my responsibility and opportunity to live my life boldly and to anchor myself and my work from a place of strength. My profession, mission and vocation call me to do so, and to help clear the path for those who will follow me.

REFERENCES

Badgett, M. V. L., Waaldijk, K., & Meulen Rodgers, Y. V. D.(2019). The relationship between LGBT inclusion and economic development: Macro-level evidence, *World Development, 120*, 1–14, https://doi.org/10.1016/j.worlddev.2019.03.011

Bernstein, R. S., Bulger, M., Salipante, P., & Weisinger, J. Y. (2020). From diversity to inclusion to equity: A theory of generative interactions. *Journal of Business Ethics, 167*, 395–410. https://doi.org/10.1007/s10551-019-04180-1

Carmichael, T. R. (2023). A quare theory analysis of black gay men college students at predominantly white institutions, *International Journal of Qualitative Studies in Education*. DOI: 10.1080/09518398.2023.2178686

Collins, S. E., Clifasefi, S. L., Stanton, J., The Leap Advisory Board, Straits, K. J. E., Gil-Kashiwabara, E., Rodriguez Espinosa, P., Nicasio, A. V., Andrasik, M. P., Hawes, S. M., Miller, K. A., Nelson, L. A., Orfaly, V. E., Duran, B. M., & Wallerstein, N. (2018). Community-based participatory research (CBPR): Towards equitable involvement of community in psychology research. *The American Psychologist, 73*(7), 884–898. https://doi.org/10.1037/amp0000167

Conron, K. J., O'Neill, K. K., & Marzulio, M. A. (2022). *Community college and the experiences of lgbtq people.* Williams Institute, University of California at Los Angeles, School of Law. https://williamsinstitute.law.ucla.edu/publications/community-college-lgbtq/

Crenshaw, K. (1989). Demarginalizing the intersection of race and sex: A black feminist critique of antidiscrimination doctrine, feminist theory and antiracist politics. *University of Chicago Legal Forum, 1*(8), 139–167. https://chicagounbound.uchicago.edu/uclf/vol1989/iss1/8

Denizet-Lewis, B. (2003). Double lives on the downlow. *New York Times.* https://www.nytimes.com/2003/08/03/magazine/double-lives-on-the-down-low.html

Duran, A. (2018). Queer and of color: A systematic literature review on queer students of color in higher education scholarship, *Journal of Diversity in Higher Education, 12*(4), 390–400. http://dx.doi.org/10.1037/dhe0000084

Ellis, K. E. (2023). "What we do have, we can polish": Towards quare placemaking in lgbtq+ student affairs. *The Vermont Connection, 44*(1). https://scholarworka.uvm.Edu/tvc/vol44/iss1/6

Epstein, R. M. (1999). Mindful practice. *JAMA, 282*(9), 833–839. https://doi.org/10.1001/jama.282.9.833

Garvey, J. C., Mobley, S. G., Jr., Summerville, K. S., & Moore, G. T. (2019). Queer and trans* students of color: navigating identity disclosure and college contexts, *The Journal of Higher Education, 90* (1), 150–178, DOI: 10.1080/00221546.2018.1449081

Gasman, M., Abiola, U., & Travers, C. (2015). Diversity and senior leadership at elite institutions of higher education. *Journal of Diversity in Higher Education, 8*(1), 1–14. https://psycnet.apa.org/doi/10.1037/a0038872

Goldberg, A. E., Beemyn, G. & Smith, J. Z. (2019). What is needed, what is valued: Trans students' perspectives on trans-inclusive policies and practices in higher education. *Journal of Educational and Psychological Consultation. 29*(1). 27–67. https//: doi.org/10.1080/10 8474412.2018.1480376

Harper, S. R., & Simmons, I. (2018). *Black students at public colleges and universities: A 50-state report card.* https://www.luminafoundation.org/wp-content/uploads/2018/09/black-students-at-public-colleges-and-universities.pdf

Hartocollis, L., Solomon, P., Doyle, A., & Ditty, M. (2015). An evaluation of the university of Pennsylvania's practice doctorate (DSW) program. *Journal of Teaching in Social Work, 35* (1–2), 116–130. DOI: 10.1080/08841233.2014.980487.

Henry, S. (2021). Critical engagement: Lessons learned and implications for hrd about black male faculty leadership in higher education. *Advances in Developing Human Resources, 23*(4), 300–318. DOI: 10.1177/15234223211037750

Human Rights Campaign Foundation. (2021a). *The state of mental health and lgbtq communities of color.* https://hrc-prod-requests.s3-us-west-2.amazonaws.com/assets/BIPOC-Mental-Health-LGBTQ-2021.pdf

Human Rights Campaign Foundation. (2021b). *An epidemic of violence: fatal violence against transgender and gender non-confirming people in the United States in 2020.* https://reports.hrc.org/an-epidemic-of-violence-fatal-violence-against-transgender-and-gender-non-confirming-people-in-the-united-states-in-2020?_ga=2.232280927.1313483102.1692226231-224502038.1690819071

Johnson, E. P. (2001). "Quare" studies, or (almost) everything I know about queer studies I learned from my grandmother, *Text and Performance Quarterly*, *21*(1), 1–25, DOI: 10.1080/10462930128119

Lesnick, A. S. (2021). Exploring the need for and benefits of lgbtqa faculty and staff groups in higher education. *LGBT Policy Journal*, *11*(1). https://lgbtq.hkspublications. org/2021//06/11/exploring-the-need-for-and-benefits-of-lgbtqa-faculty-and-staff-groups-in-higher-education/

Lovett, I. (2013). After 37 years of trying to change people's sexual orientation, group is to disband. *New York Times*. https://www.nytimes.com/2013/06/21/us/group-that-promoted-curing-gays-ceases-operations.html

Means, D. R., & Jaeger, A. J. (2013). Black in the rainbow: "Quaring" the black gay male student experience at historically Black universities. *Journal of African American Males in Education (JAAME)*, *4*(2), 124–140.

Meyer, I. (2003). Prejudice, social stress, and mental health in lesbian, gay, and bisexual populations: Conceptual issues and research evidence. *American Psychological Association*, *129*(5). DOI: 10.1037/0033-2909.129.5.674

National Association of Social Workers. (2021). *Code of ethics of the National Association of Social Workers*. https://www.socialworkers.org/About/Ethics/Code-of-Ethics/ Code-of-Ethics-English

Papadimitriou, A. (2020). Beyond rhetoric: Reinventing the public mission of higher education. *Tertiary Education and Management*, *26*(1). 1–4. https://doi.org/10.1007/ s11233-019-09046-9

Robinson, B. A. (2021). "They peed on my shoes": Foregrounding intersectional minority stress in understanding LGBTQ youth homelessness, *Journal of LGBT Youth*, DOI: 10.1080/19361653.2021.1925196

Schneider, B., Ehrhart, M. G., & Macey, W. H. (2013). Organizational climate and culture. *Annual Review of Psychology*, *64*(1), 361–388. doi:10.1146/annurev-psych-113011-143809

Scott, D. (2021). Stigma in place: Black gay men's experiences of the rural South. *Health & place*, *68*, 102515. https://doi.org/10.1016/j.healthplace.2021.102515

Shange, N. (1975). *For colored girls who considered suicide when the rainbow is enuf.* Scribner Poetry

The Trevor Project.(2022). *Homelessness and housing instability among LGBTQ youth*. https://www.thetrevorproject.org/wp-content/uploads/2022/02/Trevor-Project-Homelessness-Report.pdf

VIGNETTE ONE

OVERCOMING ADVERSITY AS A MALE BLACK DOCTORAL PHARMACY STUDENT

Aaron Hargrove

As a Black, gay, male doctoral pharmacy student, my journey has been filled with challenges and triumphs. From the beginning, I have faced numerous obstacles that tested my determination and perseverance. However, these challenges have only fueled my desire to prove to myself and the world that anything is possible. In this vignette, I want to share my experiences, the challenges I faced, and how I persevered through it all.

Being a Black man in a predominantly white field like pharmacy has not always been easy. I have often encountered stereotypes and biases that hindered my progress and ability to shine fully. However, rather than succumbing to these negative perceptions, I embraced them as motivation to excel. I was determined to prove to myself and others that I was capable and talented, regardless of my race or background.

Being a doctoral pharmacy student requires dedication and sacrifice. The rigorous coursework, research projects, and exams demanded high commitment. However, this was only compounded by the fact that I was juggling my academic

The Journey: Truths of Same-Gender-Loving Black Males in Higher Education, pages 13–14.
Copyright © 2025 *Antione D. Tomlin*
Published under exclusive licence by Emerald Publishing Limited
ISBNs: 978-1-83708-498-2 HB, 978-1-83708-499-9 PB,
978-1-83708-500-2 EPDF, 978-1-83708-501-9 EPUB

responsibilities with my personal life. As a Black man, I often had to navigate societal pressures and expectations, all while ensuring that my loved ones were taken care of. This balancing act required immense discipline and time management, but I refused to let it hinder my academic pursuits.

In addition to academic obstacles, I faced social and cultural challenges as a Black male doctoral pharmacy student. From being the only Black man in my classes to being the only Black man in professional settings, I often felt isolated and alone. However, rather than succumbing to these feelings, I sought support systems and mentorship to help me navigate these challenges. I found solace in the camaraderie of other Black males in the profession, who shared similar experiences and understood my journey. Together, we worked tirelessly to break down barriers and create a more inclusive and diverse environment for ourselves and future generations.

The path to success is seldom a straight one. Throughout my academic journey, I encountered numerous failures and setbacks. However, instead of letting them discourage me, I embraced them as opportunities for growth and learning. Each mistake or obstacle I encountered was a stepping stone towards my eventual success. I learned to view failure as a valuable lesson that would shape me into a more resilient and determined individual.

As a Black male doctoral pharmacy student, I have always aimed to prove to myself and the world that anything is possible. Through determination, perseverance, and unwavering belief in myself, I have overcome countless obstacles and achieved success beyond my expectations. My journey has reminded me that adversity is a part of life, but how we respond to it defines us. By continuing to excel and breaking barriers, I hope to inspire other Black males to pursue their dreams and to realize that they, too, can overcome any adversity that comes their way.

In conclusion, my experience as a Black, gay, male doctoral pharmacy student has been challenging and rewarding. I have faced numerous obstacles, but these challenges have only fueled my determination to succeed. By embracing failure as a learning opportunity, finding support systems, and proving to myself and the world that anything is possible, I have overcome adversity and achieved remarkable success. My journey is a testament to the power of resilience, determination, and the belief that anything can be achieved with the right mindset.

NARRATIVE TWO

OBSCURITY OF BLACK GAY MALES IN ACADEMIC WORKPLACES

Kelly Wallace[1]

Drexel University

In many ways academic settings are rooted in heterosexual identities. Likewise, there is an overwhelming dominance of white culture which have sustained barriers to people of color not only being in these spaces, but also being able to operate authentically. Specifically, when addressing the intersecting needs of being Black and Gay, it is often overlooked or even ignored in academia spaces. Often many colleagues in higher education do not share these identities and lived experiences. Black Gay men often experience isolation and roadblocks within their educational profession. And there are minimal to not supportive systems to support a healthy work/life balance. The purpose of this chapter is to share my story as a Black Gay male educator, present successes, and challenges along my journey in academia and, provide recommendations to promote and strengthen an inclusive work environment for Black Gay men.

[1] k.wallace25@yahoo.com

The Journey: Truths of Same-Gender-Loving Black Males in Higher Education, pages 15–22.
Copyright © 2025 *Antione D. Tomlin*
Published under exclusive licence by Emerald Publishing Limited
ISBNs: 978-1-83708-498-2 HB, 978-1-83708-499-9 PB,
978-1-83708-500-2 EPDF, 978-1-83708-501-9 EPUB

Key Words: Colleges and Universities, Academia, Imposter Syndrome, Black Men, Gay Men

OBSCURITY OF BLACK GAY
MALES IN ACADEMIC WORKPLACES

My Journey into Academia

Growing up in a family where every person and couple identified as heterosexual instilled an early belief that I was different. As I continued to grow, I soon learned who I truly was. If you are wondering, yes, I knew I was Gay in adolescent. Throughout elementary and secondary school I had teachers who shared my racial identity. However, most of these professionals were women; I only had one Black male teacher. Entering college, I attended a Historically Black College & University (HBCU) and met and interacted with Black professionals in various stages of their careers. It was here that birthed my thought of going into academia professionally. During my senior year I enrolled in a course which required me to take the role of a teaching assistant.

As a teaching assistant I was provided the opportunity to learn directly from faculty, develop and facilitate lectures and other classroom activities, grade assignments, and hold office hours. While there were Black male educators in the department, at the time I was the only male teaching assistant. At the same time, I was also the only Gay teaching assistant as well. In short, this solidified my goal of being an educator. I knew I not only wanted to be in the space of academia but that because of who I am I was needed to shift the dominate narrative which promotes heterosexual individuals as being the majoring in academic settings.

After completing my master's and searching for doctoral programs to apply to, I immediately knew one of my goals for pursuing this advanced degree was to teach. A phrase I often refer to when people ask me why I want to earn a doctorate is: "this degree is my seat at the table; it is my key to be in spaces which were not designed to include those who are me and operate like me". This phrase represents what it means to me to be a Black Gay male in academia.

Black and Queer in Academia

In truth, being a Black Gay male in academia, for me, is a stance and opportunity for change. Within the academic realm there are already a limited amount of Black male educators and even less Black Gay males. This underrepresentation perpetuates that we are not qualified enough or do not possess the same expertise as white and heterosexual individuals do. In my experience being both a Black and Gay male and in academia is troublesome at times. The lack of representation, limited supportive resources, and internalized self-doubt all have arisen in my experience as an educator.

Despite this, it is these experiences and beliefs that have allowed me to blossom into an amazing educator. Over time I have learned to use my discomfort as a driving force to push me to go further. For example, I taught a graduate level family therapy class where most of my students identified as White, among other identities. As a Black Gay educator, I used not only the curriculum but also my identity and experiences personally and professionally to teach my students the importance of race and race related issues in the mental health field. Of course, some educators can argue that self-disclosure is inappropriate or unnecessary in the educational journey. However, Blumer et al.(2013) described how often in family therapy programs, teaching occurs from a cisgender framework which limits students understanding of gender and gender identities.

This is exactly my point. Coming from two communities which are collectivist and not individualistic allows me to create an atmosphere of inclusion. My students felt safe sharing difficult stories and moments they have experienced as it related to the course content. This maintained a classroom environment which promoted self-discovery. My students uncovered biases, assumptions, and belief systems that could impact their work with diverse communities such as people of color (POC) and the lesbian, gay, bisexual, transgender, queer or questioning, intersex, asexual, and more (LGBTQIA+). Again, this goes back to what it means to be a Black Gay male in academia; to be someone who dismantles false narratives and shapes the academic experience as a village where students learn not only from me, but also through their interactions with each other. This creates an opportunity to reflect and develop true cultural competency.

Imposter vs. Me

Based on my experience one of the most challenging things about being a Black Gay male in higher education is the imposter syndrome. Imposter syndrome, at one point, took over most of the elements of my life. Imposter syndrome has been defined as the experience of second guessing or doubt about one's skills, achievements, or abilities and continuous internalized fear and anxiousness about how one is perceived (Sverdlik et al., 2020). While there are many items connected to my experience of imposter syndrome the most prevalent was the lack of visibility. What I mean by this is within many academic spaces there was a lack of both Black men and same gender loving Black men. Being a Black male in academia I often felt that I would be perceived or evaluated different by both other faculty and students. Then, being a Black Gay male further perpetuated my concern that I couldn't bring my wholeness into academic spaces in fear of judgement or discrimination.

The prior statement is not meant to be a sad story but further highlights how my doubtfulness and a sense of inability was sustained due to the lack of representation in both respective fields. Furthermore, being in academic settings where I did not have anyone who shared my identities, I became entrapped in my own negative thoughts. At the time, I did not realize that I was experiencing imposter syndrome and did my best to push through. This "pushing through" would ulti-mately lead me to doubt my skills as a professional, doctoral student, mentor, and many other areas of my life. I began to question if I was qualified enough to be in a doctoral program, which caused me to compare my skills and accomplishments with those of my peers. This further led me to question my abilities as a therapist and educator; my peers also shared these roles. And since I began to believe I wasn't good enough, my ability to perform in these roles declined. Also, I recog-nized that I began to operate as someone I was not in an effort to demonstrate I was "good enough".

However, once I allowed myself permission to return to my authentic self, I rediscovered the power of my voice. And I rediscovered how much others appre-ciated and became powerful, in their own way, through the power of my voice. For example, I have heard from several clients throughout my career as a therapist that they appreciate the safe and inviting space I create in therapy. A client once shared with me that she really enjoyed how I helped her believe in herself and stop doubting who she was. Similarly, as a professor students have told me that they really enjoyed my approach to teaching and my ability to make students feel comfortable being themselves. One student specifically shared that after taking my class she felt so much more comfortable discussing issues of race with her clients. As I allowed these and other memories to flood my mind I became even more of my genuine self and my functionality overall improved.

Rediscovering My Voice

The rediscovery of my voice allowed me to become the greatest version of my authentic self I have ever experienced. Beyond being a doctoral candidate, I also have positions as an instructor, therapist, and mentor. When I first began my posi-tion as a professor, I was myself. I was strong, determined, and motivated to pro-mote change. Promoting change through teaching students not only curriculum, but also how to allow their authentic self to be present in their future ambitions. However, what I didn't recognize at the time was I wasn't allowing my full self to come through. For example, I would often think about how students perceived me as a loving Black Gay male. I would never hide this fact as again representa-tion mattered to me. But I would wonder things such as: "Am I good enough?". "What can I offer these students?". "Am I as qualified as other faculty?". "What if I mess up?". Overtime, these thoughts built up to block my ability to fully be my authentic self. Eventually, this led me to begin believing I was an imposter.

In rediscovering my voice, I was reminded of the person I am and the impor-tance of being my authentic self. These reminders came in the form of self-reflec-tion and affirmations. I recall going back to rereading my acceptance letter for my doctoral program. I was reminded of why I desired to work in academia and the change I hoped to enact. I also began journaling my success stories as a professor, therapist, and other areas of my life. This helped to serve as a constant reminder of my abilities. Additionally, I allowed others to pour into my self-esteem. This looked like embracing the positive feedback I would hear from both students and clients. For example, accepting the strengths that faculty, supervisors, colleagues, and others would often share with me. Whereas before, I would hear the positive attributes others would share about me but would continue to compare myself to others. So, being my authentic self means several things but the most important element of this is being Kelly. Being Kelly looks like being warm, inviting, insightful, consistent, and defeating stereotypes. One of the many ways I define myself is Black and Gay or Black and Queer. These two identities speak volumes to me personally but also to me as a professional. Every space I enter these identities are center to my presence. Specifically, in academic settings I often share my identities with students and colleagues to promote an inclusive educational environment and acknowledge that diversity goes beyond classroom curriculum.

SOLUTION FOCUS APPROACH

Progress continues to be made in academic spaces to acknowledge and honor the diversity of students such as race, religion/spirituality, gender, gender identity, sexuality, sexual orientational, national origin, etc. Some examples of this inclusion include campus festivities/ activities, peer mentoring, holidays, cultural events, showcases and workshops to highlight diversity of students across campus (Eakins & Eakins, 2017). This is done both to recruit diverse students and ensure they feel embraced during their academic journey. Like these events, similar strides are being made to recognize the diversity of faculty and staff. For example, luncheons, email blasts, and other events to show appreciation for the campus community. However, what is often missed is intersectionality or having multiple identities.

Being a Black and Gay male are two identities, each of which comes with their own experience of oppression, discrimination, and invisibility in academic settings. For example, heterosexual faculty and staff don't have to consider or be worried about displaying photographs of their partner or spouse. Whereas members of the LGBTQIA+ community can potentially face backlash from other faculty, staff, and students. Members of these communities could face retaliation in the form of lack of promotion or possible termination. Similarly, POC often face daily microaggressions in academic environments. This could look like hurtful phrases about POC or negative interpretation about POC displaying assertiveness. These circumstances increase workplace stress, anxiety, and self-doubt.

In my experience, workplace stress is normal, especially being in academia. Managing courseloads, grading, office hours, meetings, etch can be enormous tasks on a tight schedule. However, lacking representation as a Black Gay male brings into context self-doubt which can intensify stress into anxiety. Additionally, extending beyond the classroom space there are struggles that my communities/identities face ranging from access to healthcare, violence, and equitable wages. Compiling all these elements together creates internalized and externalized pressures that academic spaces are often blind to and not equipped to effectively manage.

Solution-Focus Not Problem-Focused

When discussing topics of racism and homophobia in academic settings there sometimes are spaces where faculty and staff can meet and discuss the direct and indirect impact of these issues. Colleges and universities may invite a guest speaker to host a discussion on these topics. This individual or sometimes a group of individuals may be represented as experts on these topics or have a wealth of knowledge in these areas. Sometimes faculty members in these communities are asked to host these lectures/discussions for their colleagues. While these opportunities do help provide a space for these discussions, this is often where they stop.

While discussing these challenges is important; often there are not identified next steps or solutions to eliminate or reduce these challenges. Academic settings may have explored resources to help decrease the presence or impact of racism and homophobia but minimally develop and implement long-term strategies. This could be due to several factors including funding, staffing, hierarchy of needs, etc. However, to promote an inclusive academic environment for faculty and staff, those in leadership must develop and integrate effective strategies to ensure elongated inclusive environments. Some ways in which this can be done are through benefits and coverage, recruitment and retention, and work-life balance.

Benefits & Coverage

Many higher education positions such as Associate or Assistant professors are offered packages which offer different benefits. These benefits may provide coverage for health, dental, life insurance, and retirement plans for faculty and staff. Their spouse and/or children may be eligible to also receive coverage through these benefit packages. Similarly, depending on the position and length of employment some additional benefits may include some sort of tuition stipend or reimbursement for their spouse or children should they seek furthering their education. However, often these benefits may not be applicable to same-sex couples. This employment inequity can leave same gender loving faculty and staff and their partners forced to find other methods of coverage. To promote inclusive working environments, higher education settings must utilize benefits plans that provide coverage for same gender loving couples. This will reduce same gender loving faculty and staff from experiencing workplace discrimination and promote inclusiveness of the academic field.

Marketing, Recruitment, and Retention

Many times, during advertisement of academic positions there are diversity, equity, and inclusion statements which promotes that the specific placement will not discriminate against potential employees based on race, gender, sexuality, and many other identities and characteristics. In addition to these statements, if there are advertisements which feature same gender loving faculty and staff in the workplace this can showcase how inclusive the work environment is. For example, on the main college or university website or in another publication or promotional material, featuring a Black Gay male faculty or staff member can help members of these communities feel a sense of security and support when considering employment. Additionally, spotlighting work, research, publications, teaching, and other accomplishments by Black and Gay faculty or staff members demonstrates the academic settings commitment to diversity.

Furthermore, as mentioned before many of these institutions have discussions and conversations about issues related to race and sexuality. However, there is minimal solutions provided when same gender loving Black men experience discrimination both on and off campus. For example, an instructor being addressed by a student or colleague in a negative way. Or a staff member who is experiencing distress due to policies around same-sex marriage. These events often invoke difficult emotions and impact one's ability to perform at their best. Therefore, offering a safe and affirming spaces to support Black Gay men can ensure a healthy work-life balance but also help retain these individuals who may consider terminating their position otherwise. An example of this could be hiring a mental health professional who specializes in issues of racism and sexuality discrimination. This can be the space for faculty and staff to discuss and develop strategies to manage emotions.

Workplace Culture

Many higher education spaces are dominated by White culture (Haynes ,2017). White culture often promotes values and customs that are not connected to the Black male experience. This also promotes narratives surrounding heterosexism which intensifies internalized homophobia. While others within white culture will likely experience successful relationship forming, alliance building, and cooperation. This can contribute to Black and Gay employees experiencing anxiety or depression because of the workplace culture.

An opportunity to reduce the dominance of white culture includes encouraging community members to display Pride flags. Or promoting informational materials such as academic newsletters, blogs, and other materials which share information and resources surrounding race and homosexuality with all campus faculty and staff. Additionally, developing and maintaining workshops and other interventions which educate and promote diversity can increase cultural competency amongst all faculty and staff (Luster-Edward & Martin, 2018). According to Riggs et al., (2011) the more knowledge and exposure higher education professionals have about homosexuality, the less likely negative attitudes are to manifest.

In summary, being a same gender loving Black male or a Black Gay male, as I often identify by, is at the forefront of my everyday life. These identities impact the way I believe in myself; my passion for my work; and my ability to interact and connect with others. Unfortunately, as many of my fellow Black Gay men have experienced hardships, so have I. Those difficult moments I have shared in this work are an overview of my experience of being in higher education. However, as difficult as these moments were, they did not overshadow the positive experiences and outcomes I have had. And it is these great moments which have helped shape my ability to be my full authentic self. The recommendations that were discussed are but a few that can help restructure the barriers to same gender loving Black males being their authentic selves in higher education. A final reminder, things are forever changing and the experience of same gender loving Black men is unique. To maintain the cultural value, knowledge, and expertise we bring into academic spaces, these institutions must be flexible and adaptable to honor our uniqueness.

REFERENCES

Blumer, M. L., Gavriel, A. Y., & Watson, C. M. (2013). Cisgenderism in family therapy: how everyday clinical practices can delegitimize people's gender self-designations. *Journal of Family Psychotherapy, 24,* 267–285.

Eakins, A., & Eakins Sr, S. L. (2017). African American students at predominantly White institutions: A collaborative style cohort recruitment & retention model. *Journal of Learning in Higher Education, 13*(2), 51–57.

Haynes, C. (2017). Dismantling the White supremacy embedded in our classrooms: White faculty in pursuit of more equitable educational outcomes for racially minoritized students. *International Journal of Teaching and Learning in Higher Education, 29*(1), 87–107.

Luster-Edward, S., & Martin, B. (2018). Minorities in higher education in the united states: their status and disparities in student and faculty representation in a midwest research i university. *Higher Education Studies, 9.* 68. 10.5539/hes.v9n1p68.

Riggs, A. D., Rosenthal, A. R., & Smith-Bonahue, T. M. (2011). The impact of a combined cognitive–affective intervention on pre-service teachers' attitudes, knowledge, and anticipated professional behaviors regarding homosexuality and gay and lesbian issues. *Teaching and Teacher Education, 27,* 201–209.

Sverdlik, A., Hall, N. C., & McAlpine, L. (2020). PhD imposter syndrome: Exploring antecedents, consequences, and implications for doctoral well-being. *International Journal of Doctoral Studies, 15,* 737–758.

VIGNETTE TWO

THE BLACK, BI, MALE EXPERIENCE

Anthony Davis

Being a Black bisexual male in undergrad was filled with timeless moments. I met some amazing people who would support me and my journey without a blink of an eye. Often confused with me being gay, I had to constantly educate people on what bisexuality is to which I say, knowledge is power. My social status never changed in my eyes with people knowing about me which was a blessing. My first roommate was gay and our bond throughout undergrad and even until this day is by far second to none. I gained a brother and he made my experience so much more fun and with purpose. I love being a Black bisexual male and I love the skin I'm in.

The Journey: Truths of Same-Gender-Loving Black Males in Higher Education, page 23.
Copyright © 2025 *Antione D. Tomlin*
Published under exclusive licence by Emerald Publishing Limited
ISBNs: 978-1-83708-498-2 HB, 978-1-83708-499-9 PB,
978-1-83708-500-2 EPDF, 978-1-83708-501-9 EPUB

NARRATIVE THREE

IT WASN'T JUST A PHASE

Desmond Dunklin

Life experiences afford us the opportunity to learn who we are from those experiences to help contribute to our personal growth. I often heard people say that college is not for me, and I completely agree school is not for everyone, however it was my college experiences that contributed to the person that I am. I was a small country boy from the South. I started my undergrad degree in 2011 at a small Southern Baptist University. Now let me just say this, being from the country and transitioning to the big city was a complete cultural shock for me. There was always something to do, or some place to go. I was forty five minutes away from the beach in every direction, and an hour and a half from New Orleans. That's right you heard me Nola babeeee (New Orleans Accents). Oh the times I had in that city.

The friends that you meet in college, will become lifelong friends. These are the people that you lean in in times of need, the people that you navigate the next four years of your life with. These people will ultimately help you on your journey to becoming the person you are meant to be. When I got to college, I didn't know what I wanted to major in, all I knew was that I wanted to be in a field where I was helping people. I have always been a nurturer and a giver. Some would say that's just the Capricorn in me. So I decided to major in pre-med. Now hunni listen, I don't know what I was thinking but I stuck with it for the first semester.

The Journey: Truths of Same-Gender-Loving Black Males in Higher Education, pages 25–30.
Copyright © 2025 *Antione D. Tomlin*
Published under exclusive licence by Emerald Publishing Limited
ISBNs: 978-1-83708-498-2 HB, 978-1-83708-499-9 PB,
978-1-83708-500-2 EPDF, 978-1-83708-501-9 EPUB

Now the institution that I went to was a very small Predominantly White Institution (PWI) with only about 1,500 students. So all of the Black students knew each other. So it wasn't hard to connect with other people that looked like you. I was in choir when I met my best friend. We are auditioning for sections in the choir. He asked me what I was, I told him I was a tenor. He said so am I. I replied with no, I think you are a bass. He was like how are you going to tell me what I am? So I auditioned, and was told to go to the tenor section. He auditioned, and was told to go to the bass. I gave him this look like, Told you bitch, and we just chuckled. From that moment on we connected and we talked every day. Now, but my best friend was not straight in any capacity. He knew he was gay and everybody at the entire university knew. He wore hoochie daddy shorts before people knew what hoochie daddy shorts were. However, I respected the person that he was as long as he knew that I was like that. In my mind, I was still straight and nobody was going to tell me any different. That was until my friend found out about my tea. That right he caught the doll. Back then we had BGC (Black Gay Chat) and Adam 4 Adam that was before the Grindr & Jack'd apps surfaced.So my best friend found out and cornered me in the cafe, and flat out said, so this is you, and of course I couldn't lie. So what did I do? I started crying. Now let's call a spade a spade, I didn't know what I was doing back then. I was young, I was experimenting. I was still dating and having sex with girls. I hung with the gays and the straight boys. I always believed in keeping my personal life and private life separate because I didn't know who I was or what I was becoming. All I knew was that I had feelings for both sexes.

My best friend helped me navigate those feelings. He talked to me about what I was feeling, and he supported me however I chose to live my life, without judgment. When you navigate these feelings of trying to find out who you are as a same gender loving individual, a strong support system of people who love you, support you, but most of all respect your choices of how you live your life is important. I was not out during that time. I was still living my life in secret.

By this time, I had decided to go into the field of education to become a teacher. Being a black male educator is a rewarding career choice, however being a black male educator and being a homosexual man presented many challenges. I always feared the judgment of people finding out about my sexuality. I was certified in kindergarten-6th grade. One of the things that I feared was people finding out about my sexuality because there are people who think because you enjoy the company of a man that you look at children, and that was something I have always feared. So I continued to live my life in secret. I kept my personal life and private life separate.

I transitioned into higher education in 2021. I have always wanted to work in higher education. My college experiences shaped who I am. I was able to find out who I was, but more importantly who I am meant to become. Higher education today is different from what I remembered in college. The kids are not hiding in the shadows any more. They are living their life with rainbow flags, boots, bangles and more and they don't care who knows. There are resources now that support the LGBTQ+ community. Resources that were not available when I was in college to help support the transition in becoming who you really want to be. After seeing this, I was done hiding. I was done living my life in secret.

STEPPING OUT OF THE SHADOWS

My first challenge that I faced was seeing one of my students downtown at the drag show. I was with my frat brother and some other Black male educators enjoying the drag show. As I walked up to tip one of the girls, my student spotted me dead in my tracks. He came and spoke, and stated how happy he was to see me. Of course he mentioned how he always thought I was one of the girls but he didn't want to be disrespectful and approach me in that manner. I immediately corrected him, and stated I was one of the boys, let just be clear. We chatted, laughed, and talked for a minute and then I went back to enjoying myself with my friend. About three weeks later that same student came into my office, and he asked if he could talk to me. I wasn't prepared for the conversation that was about to take place. However, he was my student, and I was open to helping any way that I could. He began to cry, and I asked what was wrong, and he began to explain how his parents were not supportive of his lifestyle, and how he felt alone and that he didn't have anyone to talk to about this lifestyle and navigate the experiences of being a same gender loving individual. At that moment, I found myself at a crossroad, do I create professional boundaries and refer him to the LGBTQ+ center for resources, or do I listen. So I chose to listen. Then I begin to share my own experiences of how I had to navigate the same journey, and how I am currently till this day still navigating this journey. After we finished talking, he left my office, and I broke down in tears. I didn't know why I was crying, all I knew was that I made an impact on a student that day. I was walking in my purpose of being an educator, a mentor, a guide for this young man. These weren't tears of sadness but tears of joy. I called my best friend afterwards, and shared the experience. My best friend told me these words, " Your purpose is greater than your sexuality, you have the chance to be a guide to people who look like you, who walk like you , but more importantly who love the same way that you do. So walk in it. Be the resource because it is so easy for kids to get lost in this world without a mentor that they can look up to and feel comfortable sharing their experiences with". At that very moment, I was filled with joy because I had helped someone find their way.

YOU'RE NEVER ALONE

As you continue to grow as a professional, you meet colleagues that are navigating this thing called life just as well as you are. Post Pandemic, my friends and I were outside, and when I say we were outside we were outside outside. So we took a trip to NOLA babeee for the Red Dress Run. The Red Dress Run is a charity run in New Orleans that raises awareness for various cancers and heart disease. So my friends and I are in the streets with our red dresses on having a good ol time, when low and behold, I ran into one of my colleagues who was there with his partner. This colleague and I work in the same Division of Student Affair at our institution. So imagine my surprise when I found out that he was a same gender loving Black man as I was. We held conversations, he introduced his partner, we took a few shots, and had a good time. This exchange showed me that you can live your life, live your dream, and have that special someone to share all of the precious memories that life has to offer. Once we returned, we had lunch and discussed the weekend, and discussed life as same gender loving Black men in higher education. We discussed our fears of being open in the environment we work in. During our lunch, he made a statement, that I am living for me and not anyone else. That statement rang in my spirit for days. Why was I hiding? Why was I scared to live my life without regrets? Why was I afraid to love? I experienced puppy love before during my undergraduate years in college.

During my sophomore year of college, I stayed in an all boys residence hall. The men's basketball team, track team, and soccer team all stayed in this dorm. That is where I met him. He was 6'0 ft tall, 145lb and he ran track. I used to work at the local campus dining option called Grille Works. He and some of the other track boys would come in after practice every day, and he would order the same things, chicken tenders tossed in buffalo sauce, curly fries, mozzarella sticks, and a blue PowerAde. We would make small talk when his boys walked off. We would work out together, go to the gym and sporting events together and we became very good friends. Everything changed during Fall break, we were on campus for Fall break because he ran track and I did stats for the men's basketball team so we had to stay. We hung out, watched movies like we normally did, had a few drinks, and then he said man I love you bro. I responded with bro I love you too. He was like no bro, like I really love you, and then he got up, walked over and kissed me. Everything changed, feelings that I never felt before surfaces, emotions were running crazy, and then it just happened. It was natural, it was authentic, and it was real. We had a very extrinsic Fall Break and it continued through the Spring until he transferred. This wasn't just a phase for me, I felt something was different. I felt an attraction for him, but for me as well. This wasn't just a phase for me anymore, this was who I was, and I had to be real with myself and my feelings.

After my colleagues and I had those conversations, everything changed for me when I turned thirty. I have always been a giver, cheerleader, provider, counselor, mentor, and confidant for everyone. My family, my friends, my students, my loved one, all leaned on me in some capacity. I wasn't living for me, I was existing and living for everyone else. So after I came back from my 30th birthday trip, I sought the guidance of a therapist, who helped me sort out my feelings and emotions when it came to my life, my career, my relationship, but most of all my sexuality. I was able to deal with my feelings of being a same gender loving black man. I also learned how to love myself. I learned to accept myself for who I was and not be ashamed of myself for loving who I love regardless of gender.

STANDING ON YOUR TRUTH

Over the past year, I have attended several conferences, where I have met same gender loving men, who are also struggling to be themselves and navigate the higher education experience as a same gender loving Black man. I am constantly running into students on my own campus who are also struggling with these same issues. So I offer these three points that I have adapted to my life that have helped me navigate life in the higher education setting as a same gender loving Black man.

First, to thy own self be true. My frat brothers used to say this to me so many times, and I never understood what it meant until I started to find myself through therapy. Being true to yourself, means being able to look at yourself in the mirror and love what you see. It's being able to stand up for yourself and walk in your truth. It is also being an advocate for yourself. Oftentimes, I have seen men such as ourselves dim our light just to make others around them comfortable. Well no more. Walk in your truth and live your life. When you are true to yourself and I mean authentically true to yourself, others around you will gravitate to you. Live your life as a walking example of what living your truth really means. Being true to thy own self means accepting who you are and loving who you are regardless of what people say or how they treat you. You have to love yourself before you can love anybody else.

My second point would be your coming out is for YOU and you only. I have heard people say over and over again, I just wanna know, or why aren't you out. You are still in the closet? Are all things that I have heard from people in the community regarding my sexual preference. Noone can put you in a box or tell you how your journey is supposed to go because everyone's story is different, everyone's experience is different. For some same gender loving men, they don't have a choice of how they live their lives because living their life in secret may be better than living their life in shame, and that is ok. It is their cross to bear. I can't tell you how your journey is supposed to look, but I can support you and pray for you and encourage you to do whatever makes you happy. For me, my coming out journey is mine, and no one is going to tell me how it is supposed to look, feel, or be. So take control of your journey and do what makes you happy, whatever that may look like.

My final point is this: Pay it forward. As same gender loving men in higher education, we are in a position of influence, where we are shaping the mines of the next generation of leaders. We have experienced trials and errors, love and heartbreak, and loving our truth while trying to be the vision. It has not always been easy. Many of us have battled with depressions, thoughts of suicides, mental break downs, and identity crisis, however we have PERSEVERD, and we have have made it. So now it is our chance to pay it forward, to help lead, guide, and provide clarity to students, faculty and staff who may be feeling the pressures of being a same gender loving man in higher education. One of the things that I have learned in this thing called life is that you cannot physically, mentally, emotionally or spiritually do it all on your own. You are going to need help. With that being said, as a same gender loving Black man in higher education, be the change, be the leader, be the voice, but also be the visionary to pave the way. Nelson Mandela once stated , "Your Playing small does not serve the world, who are you not to be great".

NARRATIVE FOUR

DUOETHNOGRAPHY

Truth Telling, Differences and Commonalities in the Experiences of Two Same-Gender Loving Black Men in Academia

Andrew B. Campbell and Kaschka R. Watson

INTRODUCTION

Despite the public's view of higher education institutions being liberal and a beacon of hope for all, within the walls of the academy, many Same-Gender-Loving Black Males (SGLBM) are still faced with persistent systemic barriers and implicit biases. SGLBM face vulnerabilities because of their intersecting identities (Crenshaw, 2015; Henry et al., 2017a). In fact, SGLBM have been marginalized and stigmatized throughout history and in academic spaces (Scafidi, 2016). SGLBM faculty members become discouraged in higher education institutions when they feel like they are not accepted because of who they are and the fear of hiding an aspect of their identity because of stigmatization and discrimination (Anderson & Kanner, 2011; Scafidi, 2016). For many SGLBM faculty members, they experience their livelihoods and careers in academic workplaces being threatened with

The Journey: Truths of Same-Gender-Loving Black Males in Higher Education, pages 31–45.
Copyright © 2025 *Antione D. Tomlin*
Published under exclusive licence by Emerald Publishing Limited
ISBNs: 978-1-83708-498-2 HB, 978-1-83708-499-9 PB,
978-1-83708-500-2 EPDF, 978-1-83708-501-9 EPUB

discrimination by students, course evaluations, and by supervisor's performance evaluations (Anderson & Kanner, 2011). It is through these persistent negative homophobic blows that are levelled at SGLBM and other members of the 2SLG-BTQIA+ communities that served as a framework for us to share our lived experiences of being a SGLBM in higher education spaces.

In this self-revealing chapter, we engaged in a duoethnography methodological approach (Breault, 2016; Lyle, 2018; Sawyer & Norris, 2013, 2015) to outline our career journeys through story-telling conversations about our truths, differences, and commonalities in our experiences as SGLBM coming from Kingston, Jamaica to now living and teaching in Ontario, Canada. In each of our conversation meetings, we vividly describe how we position ourselves in higher education spaces, the challenges and rewards of academia and we highlight the importance of maintaining authenticity and identities in higher education. We offer our readers meaningful tips/strategies/recommendations that higher education institutions can employ to further support the increase representation of SGLBM in academia, and how to inspire hope and make a clarion call for advocacy. We also encourage SGLBM who reads this chapter and has the desire to be in higher education spaces to see this as we are offering ourselves as a reminder that it is also possible for them.

POSITIONALITY

Andrew: Showing up as my whole self within my work is fundamental for me as a SGLBM, born in Jamaica, receiving my primary and secondary education in the Jamaican public school system, and being trained as a teacher in the Jamaican teacher education system. I grew up in this very colonized educational system that often I found no place or space in since I was made invisible due to my sexual orientation. These are the very concerns I continue to experience and witness within higher education in Canada. This is one of the motivations for my unstinting engagement in this work to bring about increased awareness, telling our stories as SGLBM, opportunities for unlearning, and creating intentional spaces of belonging in education where we can all afford the currency to be our best selves.

Kaschka: My interest in championing anti-Black racism, diversity, inclusion, equity, and social justice work in higher education for racialized and marginalized groups stem from my lived experiences in Jamaica and North America. Living in a homophobic Jamaica where I experienced homophobia through bullying and harassment at my high school in Kingston and in my community have imprinted in me a lasting pain and the desire to make a difference for those who have experienced the same or similar acts of discrimination as I did. For me, it was difficult and heart wrenching to watch many of my SGLBM peers at school constantly being attacked, assaulted, and abused because of their sexual orientation. At times I intervened and there were times when I could not because of fear. It was even more concerning for me to witness student leaders who were my seniors and teachers that failed to speak up, speak out and stop the hate and violence that happened to SGLBM on school grounds. After finishing high school, I immigrated to the United States and completed a Bachelor's in Cross-Cultural Studies and then immigrated to Canada and completed my graduate studies. During my experiences of being a student and educator, I've witnessed the damaging impacts of discrimination that further creates barriers and marginalized students and other racialized groups, and these have helped me to speak out against discrimination in all its forms.

METHODOLOGY

In contextualizing our personal narratives, we employed a duoethonography as a qualitative approach to inquiry about our experiences as SGLBM in higher education. According to Sawyer and Norris (2013, 2015), a duoethnography methodological approach amalgamates diverse elements of reflective inquiry that involves autoethnography, autobiography, self-study, and individuals' life histories. In going further, "duoethnographers often interrogate the cultural contexts of autobiographical experiences with issues related to personal and professional identities" (Breault, 2016, as cited in Noreiga & Nason, 2023, p. 67). As authors recalling our stories, we juxtapose the intersections in our experiences (Noreiga & Nason, 2023) as Jamaicans/Canadians who have undergone similar challenges of homophobia and have navigated those challenges and pursued academic career paths.

All our meetings were recorded via Zoom and transcribed and discussed with each other to maintain constant interaction with the data gathered. As we relished in the comfort of a brave, safe, and loving space (Campbell & Eizadirad, 2023) that was established long ago through friendship and collegiality, we also recognized the emergent tensions and nuances that were unveiled (Breault, 2016; Sawyer & Norris, 2013, 2015) from our conversations about our experiences as SGLBM in higher education places. The unsettling emotions resurfaced the pain we felt from discrimination and being bullied in our high school and in our respective communities because we are SGLBM.

Our engagement in a duoethnography approach to our narrative analysis led to emergent themes that formed the subheadings and the conversations outlined in this chapter. Throughout the data collection and analysis processes, we ensured that we maintained the ethics of our respective experiences by speaking up and sharing our own individual stories (Lapadat, 2017) and not attempting to disclose our experiences as solely one.

ENTERING ACADEMIC SPACES AS SGLBM

Andrew: Advocacy is a crucial part of being in this space. I do not get to "live the soft life" as is said in Ghana. I understand how unsafe spaces are for me being Black, being SGLBM, and being a Jamaican immigrant. Many institutions themselves are historically and presently unsafe for me and others like me, so it is my responsibility to advocate throughout every stage of my journey. The meaning that I bring to this work and my choice to speak up, stand up, and show up are created through advocacy. #representationmatters. What does representation look like in real life, in real time, for a SGLBM?

Many times, when we enter predominantly White educational spaces, the first thing that happens to us is tokenization. When tokenizing occurs, we are watered down and controlled by systems that are designed to hire us and diminish us. This means that I must be mindful of the value I carry, the space I occupy, and my duty to self and community that I personally hold. Mentorship is another major piece of true advocacy. We know that Black males in higher education are an endangered species. We are showing up in very limited numbers. We are underrepresented. The intentionality of being a mentor in this space matters because I am not only someone who can share my lived experiences with others, but also someone who is acting by opening doors for other SGLBM.

Kaschka: I enter higher education spaces as a Black cisgender married gay man from Jamaica with ancestry ties to Africa and the Caribbean. I come to educational spaces with my lived experiences of homophobia, racism, antiblackness, anti-Black racism, and other forms of injustices that I have faced both academically and professionally. I know what it is like to be talking to students and colleagues in casual conversations or when I am socially locating myself in spaces and see the sudden changes of a welcoming smile on peoples faces to stern facial expressions when I mentioned that I am married to another SGLBM or when I make references to my husband. I acknowledge these circumstances and move on because that is who I am. I am Kaschka and I have grown to embrace me and all the beauty of my intersecting identities that make me who I am today. I am confident, loving, brave, unbothered, unique, and extraordinary. These attributes have enabled me to navigate the discriminations that made me feel "othered" and have made me even more resilient in showing up in higher education spaces as I am. These experiences have also fueled my passion for teaching and doing research in higher education that focus on diversity, inclusion, equity, anti-Black racism, anti-oppression, 2SLGBTQIA+ issues, and social justice in education for all equity deserving groups. I am new to writing about and sharing my vulnerability as a SGLBM in higher education, but I am passionate about addressing injustices that the 2SLGBTQIA+ communities experiences and by sharing my own personal stories, I am hoping that others can see themselves reflected in my story and speak about their own in their own time.

EXAMPLES THAT HELPED SHAPED WHO WE ARE AS SGLBM IN THE ACADEMY

Andrew: **Fear and Flight:** The word journey is a very dear word to me because I believe that each one of us is on a unique and individual journey through life. My journey started with fear and flight. Growing up in Jamaica, I was raised in one of the most homophobic places on the globe (Padgett, 2006). As a child, navigating this homophobic space shaped me into the person I am. These experiences not only taught me resilience, but they also taught me to resist and to love myself more. When you grow up in a space where you are not loved, chosen, or a representation of what is good, you need to find another way to carve out that goodness for yourself. People who know me realize that I am very intentional about how I carve out my own joy and create community spaces and brave spaces for others. This has shaped my work in higher education, the programs, and courses I have helped to create, and the ways I show up in spaces. Flight was embodied for me when I left Jamaica. We say that we leave for "greener pastures", and my pasture was the freedom to be and to become. I have always been a person with big dreams, and I knew that my dreams would have been stifled if I had stayed in Jamaica. I would be freer to be my whole self in a place where I was safe to express myself.

Focus and Fight. Leaving for greener pastures made me realize that other parts of my identity were now more visible and newly under attack. One of those identities was my Blackness. In Jamaica, almost everyone I interacted with was Black, but in Canada I was classified as a minority. I suddenly needed to fight back against all the microaggressions, nuances, and deficit thinking surrounding my value. I needed to fight the white gaze and being measured against white standards, especially in higher education. Black professors are seen as a deficit, and we must fight to show up as our whole selves. Terms such as "right fit" and "professionalism" are used as weapons against our ability to tell our own authentic stories and find a place of power in academia. To put Black people in research and journals where they are seen and valued and appreciated as authentic narratives is vital to our survival and strength in the academic world.

Forward and Fabulous. Amid resistance and resilience, one thing we must be very cognizant of is our celebration and enjoyment of who we are. My mind goes back to hundreds of years ago when my ancestors were dragged from the shores of Africa to the Americas as slaves, living in deeply treacherous conditions. My ancestors were still able to find joy that would sustain their physical body, emotional health, spiritual wealth, and community. Amid nothing, joy was priceless. This was evident through spirituals, singing, drumming, and food curated from nothing. I know that joy is intentional and necessary for us to not only survive but thrive in higher education. I am not here just to survive. I refused to just survive, I will thrive in academia. This is what moving forward means to me in a space that I know is intentionally filled with barriers and gatekeepers. I pay the "Black tax", but I am intentional about sitting at the front when I am expected to sit at the back. I am intentional about how I take up invitations to take a seat at the table, building my own table, speaking even when my voice trembles, showing up with pride in spaces where my identity is not prideful, and moving forward in a fabulous way despite it all. We are told as SGLBM how to turn down and remain and navigate with invisibility. We are trained not to rock the boat, especially coming from spaces in the Caribbean with a high level of hypocrisy about the existence of same-gender-loving men. We are here, we exist, we are in higher education. I will not allow myself to be silent or invisible anymore. When you see me being very visible in every space—not just at Pride—it is intentional, it is deliberate, it is a statement, it is a middle finger, it is a *f*ck you* statement. I will never be invisible again.

Kaschka: An example that helped to shape who I am as a SGLBM in higher education is my commitment to advocacy work. Advocating, especially for myself and for all equity-deserving groups have been a firm action I have always taken, going as far back as being a student in my high school in Kingston, Jamaica. As I mentioned in the former part of this chapter, even though I was a victim of homophobic bullying and have advocated for myself on many occasions, there were instances where I stood up to bullies who were bullying my SGLBM peers who felt helpless and felt like they could not stand up for themselves. I have made it my duty and reported these bullies, and I must admit that I felt fulfilled when I saw that those who inflicted harm to my SGLBM peers were held accountable for their actions. I have taken this approach to advocacy with me in the Ontario Public Service and in higher education institutions through my teaching, research, and delivering of training sessions to leaders and staff to address issues of racial inequities and social injustices. I have consistently used my voice, power, privilege and lived experiences in higher education to speak up and challenge systemic racism and all forms of discrimination that have further marginalized SGLBM and other racialized groups in academia.

My experiences collaborating with academic colleagues, especially with SGLBM on research that addressed anti-Black racism, homophobia, anti-oppression, activism and 2SLGBTQIA+ issues in higher education have helped to shaped who I am in the academy. For example, I am more invested and braver in taking on equity and social justice issues in academia, knowing that I am not alone, and that the more we as educators speak, write, and disseminate knowledge about these issues, the more higher education institutions, policymakers, and stakeholders can act to dismantle inequities and injustices in higher education. I have raised systemic issues with leadership in educational institutions and have provided them with best practices and recommendations for redressing anti-racism and (neo)colonial embedded practices in curriculum, recruitment, hiring and promotional practices. These experiences have garnered me respect among my peers, students, and senior leadership.

Being a married SGLBM has solidified who I am as an individual and in higher education spaces. I have a strong, loving, and sustainable relationship with my husband who is also Jamaican and Canadian who have supported me throughout my career and continues to do so. We have created and sustained this relationship that many from my SGLBM community do not see as a relationship that is sustainable and long-lasting because of the stereotypes that are associated with Black gay men not getting married and even if they do, their relationships are usually unsustainable or short-lived. This is further from the reality that exists for many married SGLBM in my community. I am a living proof that it is possible, and it is real. My life and the support from my husband have kept me grounded during difficult times in academia and have helped me to learn more about myself and how I engage others and my work in higher education institutions.

THE CHALLENGES AND REWARDS OF
BEING A SGLBM IN HIGHER EDUCATION

Andrew: The work to see change is hard and challenging, but we continue. The need to constantly disrupt deficit thinking is exhausting. I am committed to walking through higher education as my full authentic self, but I am also cognizant that the people around me do not see me for who I really am. People around me do not have the same dreams, hopes, ambitions and desires that I hold for myself, and this constant deficit thinking is a challenge. Because you are representing a whole group of underrepresented folks, there is a "Black tax" in higher education that says we must constantly do more. Jackson and Jones (2020) of The Education Trust explain, "It's no secret that Black people must work harder and pay more to receive the same benefits and opportunity as their white or non-Black peers. This phenomenon is commonly known as the 'Black tax'". I have been using rest as part of my resistance long before it was popular. I am intentional about my vacation, self-care, and time away. I protect my Black gay joy in unsafe spaces, which is challenging. I think back to the recent hate crime at the University of Waterloo in a gender studies classroom (Shetty, 2023). When I am by myself in quiet reflection, I have asked myself whether this could have happened to me, and the answer is a resounding yes. Do I live in fear? No. Am I cognizant of the challenges of who I am in spaces that are unsafe? Yes.

I am excited as I write this section, because as much as we talk about challenges, my journey as a SGLBM in education has been deeply rewarding. It has been rewarding to accomplish without any financial support; I have made this journey by myself. When I say, "by myself", I am referring to my drive, inspiration, motivation, and financial support needed to do this. It is equally rewarding to know that I have a community of people in my corner who are cheering me on, championing me, and showing up with their pompoms for me. It is a cycle, because another layer of the reward is how I get to show up for others. My work in advocacy has also been rewarding. I appreciate the respect I have been given for my work and my voice within many communities. I am very happy to see the spaces and the stages and the platforms on which I have been invited to share my work, voice, and lived experiences. #grateful. Grateful for allies and advocates and activists and co-conspirators and people who work with me and walk with me in solidarity. Black folks, racialized folks, and white folks who are committed to this work have all been rewarding to me.

The opportunity to work and build bridges with people who are different from me has been incredibly rewarding. Getting to unlearn from women, Indigenous folks, students, people living with disabilities, and the richly diverse people who surround me has been incredibly rewarding. Taking up space within community where I engage on boards and nonprofits that deal with 2SLGBTQIA+ communities, Black immigrants, equity seeking groups, and persons who are marginalized brings me joy. These organizations are constantly intentional around dismantling dominant ideologies and I support them in whatever way I can. Pedagogy and practice in my classroom in courses that I teach and have created and the racial and gender issues I am able to discuss is rewarding for me. Being able to do research in this area and be a part of knowledge mobilization around 2SLGBTQIA+ topics, attending conferences, and writing about our lived experiences helps me do the work. Using my voice to tell my stories and tell the stories of other SGLBM who are still fighting for equity is a powerful way to use my platform for the better.

Kaschka: A major challenge for me is not knowing whether the subtle acts of exclusions I experienced in higher education from students and colleagues are a result of my Blackness or because I am a SGLBM. There are times when I felt like I had to constantly prove myself and the legitimacy of my work compared to my white colleagues. In fact, Middleton (2016) argued that Black faculty members are given different expectations compared to their white counterparts and to gain the same recognition as their white counterparts and succeed in higher education, they must prove and sell themselves. Henry et al. (2017b) went on and expressed that, many Black faculty in the academy diligently work to prove themselves worthy of attaining tenure. My work and how I present myself and engage in the culture of higher education are always under scrutiny. This feeling fosters isolation and a lack of belonging for me as a SGLBM (Mohamed & Beagan, 2019; Watson, 2023). The fact that there are not many SGLBM in higher education spaces, makes it even more challenging to fully bring my whole self to work and for me to feel welcomed and supported by my peers and the institution. This also adds to the "chilly climate" of higher education, which is more favorable toward the dominant group (Constantine et al., 2008). Having a sense of belonging is important for me as a SGLBM in higher education and I often had to figure out the navigating strategies on my own to cope and create a sense of belonging for myself.

A proud reward for me as a SGLBM in higher education is taking time to engage in self-reflection and examining all my accomplishments thus far in academia and the impacts my works have on students, educators, institutions, and those who have a vested interest in championing equity and social justice work in higher education. Being able to contribute to scholarly works in the first year of my doctoral program and continuing that path in tackling issues of social injustices in education and adding more knowledge through different forms of dissemination like book reviews, articles, magazines, and book chapters have truly been a reward. My scholarly works have shed light on inequities and injustices in higher education and call on higher education institutions to change to practices that are more inclusive, anti-racist and equitable for all racialized and marginalized groups. It is rewarding to see students, educational leaders, institutions, and stakeholders leveraging my work and others to move the needle on equity for all and to be invited by organizations and fellow academic colleagues to be guest speakers in workplaces and in classrooms where I can share how all of us can work individually and collectively to create and nurture equitable spaces for everyone is a rewarding experience for me.

SHOWING UP IN ACADEMIA AS OUR FULL AND AUTHENTIC SELF

Andrew: Knowing who I am is the most important part of being a SGLBM in higher education, as this knowledge equips me to fully walk in my identity. I can live in my identity, own my identity, be proud of my identity, and show up authentically as my fullest self. There are so many people who look to me as a SGLBM: Black present and Black futures are both looking to me. In these spaces, I am proudly carrying the dreams, hopes, visions, and aspirations of many other Black males who aspire to enter the world of higher education. In doing so, I also carry the dreams and hopes of my ancestors with pride.

Kaschka: I present my full and authentic self in higher education spaces both as a recent graduate student and as an educator. During my graduate studies, I experienced homophobia, racism, and anti-Black racism because of my intersectionality. I have experienced discrimination because of my heavy Jamaican accent, the lack of accurate pronunciations of certain academic terminologies like trajectory, milieu, hegemony, and panacea to name a few. Despite all this, I nurtured persistency and continued to be my authentic self and not changing to blend in or to please others. Experiences like these I shared with my husband, not to resurface the pain I endured unnoticeably by those who deal the blow, but to seek solace with another SGLBM who knows and understands me, who accepts and loves me because of who I am.

As an educator, I have grown from my graduate experiences as a student, and I am now bolder, more driven, and carefree. I present my full authentic self in higher education spaces. I am not afraid to critique and challenge systemic racism that is entrenched in higher education institutions. My full and authentic self is taking on social justice issues in higher education spaces and adding knowledge and providing opportunities through my work in the field. This enables me to give voice to the voiceless, particularly to racialized and marginalized groups who quite often are not provided with the spaces and means to do so. I am who I am because I accept and know who I am and where I am heading.

Our discussions back and forth between each other about our experiences as SGLBM in higher education have made us more determined to pursue social justice work as educators. Our experiences have painted a journey that is filled with opportunities and ways in which we can work with our respective higher education institutions and others to take actions and employ recommendations that will not only support SGLBM but the 2SLGBTQIA+ communities and all faculty, students, and staff in higher education.

RECOMMENDATIONS FOR HIGHER EDUCATION TO SUPPORT SGLBM

We offer the following recommendations that higher educational institutions should take to help support the brilliance that SGLBM brings to the space; increased representation of SGLBM and Black mentorship, more opportunities for research and knowledge mobilization, fostering braver and safer spaces for SGLBM, and nurturing Black healing and joy.

Increased Black Representative and Black Mentorship Among SGLBM Faculty, Students, and Staff

The lack of representation of SGLBM have been a persistent issue in higher education spaces and there has been a lack of concrete steps taken to challenge and change the status quo (Hudson, 2014). As SGLBM teaching in higher education, we argue that SGLBM representation matters not only for faculty, but for SGLBM students and staff as well as other members of the 2SLGBTQIA+ communities. The lack of representation of SGLBM faculty, students and staff is problematic and must be addressed if higher education institutions are serious about supporting our excellence and moving the needle on equity (Watson, 2023). Representation matters and it is crucial that higher education spaces provide more programs and options for SGLBM faculty, students, and staff to take up more spaces as community. The absence of SGLBM faculty, students and staff can send a silent message that institutions are affirming our culture's heterosexism and expressing of our culture's homophobia and exclusion towards 2SLGBTQIA+ communities (Hudson, 2014). The experiences of SGLBM faculty, students, and staff are characterized through stereotypes and racism (Watson, 2023) and regardless of our achievements in higher education spaces, we continue to endure the suffering impacts of deficits and being racialized (Brooms & Davis, 2017; Mutua, 2006). Increasing the representation of SGLBM faculty, students, and staff improves their sense of belonging and the satisfaction of their experiences in higher education because they can engage and interact (Van Dyke & Tester, 2014) with peers through mentorship that share similar experiences and backgrounds.

Black mentorship plays a crucial role in SGLBM faculty success and advancement into senior leadership in higher education (Cole et al., 2017; Frazier, 2011; Holmes et al., 2007; Iheduru-Anderson, 2020; Jones et al., 2015; Jones & Osborne-Lampkin, 2013; Kamassah, 2010; Salazar, 2009; Turner et al., 1999). According to Holmes et al. (2007):

> Having a mentor of the same race/ethnicity may be optimal to establishing a cultural connection, sense of belonging, and a level of trust and communication in the

relationship. However, these same kinds of things can also be established in a cross-cultural cross-gender relationship if the ultimate goal is to provide professional development opportunities for the mentee. (p. 118)

Proving Black mentorship opportunities for SGLBM in higher education spaces creates more effective access to networks and other professional opportunities that can help them to navigate higher education (Jones et al., 2015) and foster belonging.

More Opportunities for Research and Knowledge Mobilization

Higher education spaces need to provide more opportunities for SGLBM faculty members to access research scholarships and participate in knowledge mobilization through symposiums. There is a scarcity of benefits and resources to research grants in higher education and SGLBM faculty members are pitted against each other for those limited resources. More opportunities to research funding, scholarships and knowledge mobilization will enable SGLBM faculty members to publish and disseminate their work more to help fill some of the existing gaps on issues of inequities in higher education spaces. Demonstrating how knowledge flows and why issues of inequities continue to perpetuate in higher education can help to address these challenges (Powell et al., 2018). This is also an opportunity for higher education to engage in collaborative partnerships with SGLBM faculty members and other 2SLGBTQIA+ communities "who have been historically underrepresented within, and poorly served by universities in the knowledge production process" (MacKinnon et al., 2021, p. 2). SGLBM faculty members can share their voices, incorporate Black narratives, and tell their own stories and dismantle the practice of others telling our stories. Higher education institutions who are invested in supporting SGLBM faculty members through knowledge mobilization, are creating opportunities and spaces for the younger SGLBM in academia to access knowledge that speaks about their lived experiences, histories, and intersecting identities.

Fostering Braver and Safer Spaces in Higher Education for SGLBM

Intensified hate-motivated incidents are rampant against 2SLGBTQIA+ communities and this has now made its way within the walls of higher education. The recent hate-motivated incident that led to the stabbing of three people, one of which is a faculty member in a gender studies class at the University of Waterloo (Sutton & Tucker, 2023), calls on universities to intentionally create braver and safer spaces for SGLBM faculty members and their 2SLGBTQIA+ communities. The aftermath of this incident has caused many same-gender-loving faculty members to ask themselves and each other, who is next? How are we/they are being protected? They are engaging in conversations about security and protection and how braver, more vocal, and visible they must be and to pushback by increasing their visibility. Higher education institutions must provide braver and safer spaces to cultivate relationships of trust for vulnerable groups like SGLBM and the 2SLGBTQIA+communities (Campbell & Eizadirad, 2023). For SGLBM faculty members who are also marginalized, "resistance and revolt have always been part of our existence." (Campbell & Eizadirad, 2023, p. 27). Therefore, universities need to begin with creating brave spaces as allies and work collaboratively with the same-gender-loving communities to find common ground to challenge and dismantle inequities and social injustices (Campbell & Eizadirad, 2023) and create opportunities for Black healing and joy in higher education spaces.

Nurturing Black Healing and Joy

It is important that higher education supports and nurtures SGLBM Black healing and joy from the trauma and pain they experienced through the telling of our stories. Within many academic spaces, the assuming narrative is that SGLBM and members of the 2SLGBTQIA+ community tell their stories of trauma and pain to ascertain sympathy, and this is certainly not the case. When we tell our stories we do it with intentionality and from a place of vulnerability (Campbell & Eizadirad, 2023). Yes, telling our stories is reliving the pain and trauma, but it also strengthens who we are and allow us to flourish in our identities because of our lived experiences. Higher education institutions can nurture environments that promote Black healing and joy by working in solidarity with SGLBM and other 2SLGBTQIA+ communities to make systemic changes (Campbell & Eizadirad, 2023). SGLBM are the source of their own lived experiences, and they must be supported within institutions to share their stories and to heal (Verduzco-Baker, 2018).

CONCLUSION

Overall, we argue that SGLBM are underrepresented in higher education and continue to face systemic barriers. Through a duoethnography qualitative research approach, we shared with readers our journeys from homophobic Jamaica to Canada and entering higher education spaces that are often unsafe for us as SGLBM. We shared examples that helped to shape who we are as SGLM in academia, such as being persistent and going after our dreams and using prior experiences of standing up to homophobic bullying in our high school in Kingston, Jamaica. We highlighted some of the challenges and rewards of being a SGLBM in the academy and how we continue to show up in higher education spaces as our full and authentic selves. We do this by living in and owning our identities as SGLBM, and not shying away from addressing racial injustices and inequities in higher education. We concluded the chapter by offering our readers and higher education institutions some recommendations they can employ to help them further support the excellence that SGLBM bring to academic spaces and creating opportunities for us to flourish in our identities.

REFERENCES

Anderson, K. J., & Kanner, M. (2011). Inventing a gay agenda: Students' perceptions of lesbian and gay professors. *Journal of Applied Social Psychology, 41*(6), 1538–1564.

Breault, R. A. (2016). Emerging issues in duoethnography. *International Journal of Qualitative Studies in Education, 29*(6), 777–794.

Brooms, D. R., & Davis, A. R. (2017). Staying focused on the goal: Peer bonding and faculty mentors supporting Black males' persistence in college. *Journal of Black Studies, 48*(3), 305–326.

Campbell, A. B., & Eizadirad, A. (2023). Cultivating brave spaces to take risks to challenge systemic oppression. In Eizadirad, A., Campbell, A. B., & Sider, S. (Eds.), *Counternarratives of pain and suffering as critical pedagogy: Disrupting oppression in educational contexts* (pp. 19–37). Routledge.

Cole, E. R., McGowan, B. L., & Zequera, D. D. (2017). First-year faculty of color: Narratives about entering the academy. *Equity & Excellence in Education, 50*(1), 1–12. https://doi.org/10.1080/10665684.2016.1262300.

Constantine, M. G., Smith, L., Redington, R. M., & Owens, D. (2008). Racial microaggressions against Black counseling and counseling psychology faculty: A central challenge in the multicultural counseling movement. *Journal of Counseling & Development, 86*, 348–355.

Crenshaw, K. (2015, September 24). "Why intersectionality can't wait." *Washington Post.* https://scalar.usc.edu/works/bodies/kimberl-crenshaw-why-intersectionality-cant-wait.

Frazier, K. N. (2011). Academic bullying: A barrier to tenure and promotion for African-American faculty. *Florida Journal of Educational Administration & Policy, 5*(1), 1–13.

Henry, F., Dua, E., James, C. E., Kobayashi, A., Li, P., Ramos, H., & Smith, M. S. (2017a). *The equity myth: Racialization and Indigeneity at Canadian universities.* UBC Press.

Henry, F., Dua, E., Kobayashi, A., James, C., Li, P., Ramos, H., & Smith, M. S. (2017b). Race, racialization and indigeneity in Canadian universities. *Race Ethnicity and Education, 20*(3), 300–314. https://doi.org/10.1080/13613324.2016.1260226

Holmes, S. L., Land, L. D., & Hinton-Hudson, V. (2007). Race still matters: Considerations for mentoring Black women in academe. *The Negro Educational Review, 58*(1–2), 105–129.

Hudson, J. (2014). Breaking the silence: Toward improving LGBTQ representation in composition readers. *Composition Forum, 29.* https://files.eric.ed.gov/fulltext/EJ1021995.pdf

Iheduru-Anderson, K. (2020). Barriers to career advancement in the nursing profession: Perceptions of Black nurses in the United States. *Nurs Forum, 55*, 664–677. https://doi.org/10.1111/nuf.12483

Jackson, V., & Jones, T. (2020). *The "Black Tax" is key to understanding and solving the Black student debt crisis in the time of covid-19 and beyond.* The Education Trust. https://edtrust.org/resource/the-black-tax-is-key-to-understanding-and-solving-the-black-student-debt-crisis-in-the-time-of-covid-19-and-beyond/

Jones, B., Hwang, E., & Bustamante, R. M. (2015). African American female professors' strategies for successful attainment of tenure and promotion at predominately White institutions: It can happen. *Education, Citizenship and Social Justice, 10*(2), 133–151.

Jones, T. B., & Osborne-Lampkin, L. (2013). Black female faculty success and early career professional development. *The Negro Educational Review, 64*(1–4), 59–75.

Kamassah, S. (2010). Factors that enable women of South Asian and African descent to succeed in leadership position in higher education. *College Quarterly, 13*(3), 1–17.

Lapadat, J. C. (2017). Ethics in autoethnography and collaborative autoethnography. *Qualitative Inquiry, 23*(8), 589–603.

Lyle, E. (2018). Possible selves: Resor(y)ing wholeness through autobiographical writing. *Learning Landscapes, 11*(2), 257–269.

MacKinnon, K. R., Kia, H., & Lacombe-Duncan, A. (2021). Examining TikTok's potential for community-engaged digital knowledge mobilization with equity-seeking groups. *Journal of Medical Internet Research, 23*(12), 1–10. doi: 10.2196/30315

Middleton, L. (2016). Black professors on White campuses. *The Chronicle of Higher Education.* https://www.chronicle.com/article/black-professors-on-white-campuses/

Mohamed, T., & Beagan, B. L. (2019). 'Strange faces' in the academy: Experiences of racialized and Indigenous faculty in Canadian universities. *Race Ethnicity and Education, 22*(3), 338–354. https://doi.org/10.1080/13613324.2018.1511532.

Mutua, A. (2006). *Progressive Black masculinities.* Routledge.

Noreiga, A. F., & Nason, S. M. (2023). Forging racial solidarities in education: A duoethnography of juxtaposing racial experiences. In A. Eizadirad, Z. Abawi, & A. B. Campbell (Eds.), *Enacting anti-racist and activist pedagogies in teacher education: Canadian perspectives* (pp. 63–81). Canadian Scholars.

Padgett, T. (2006). The most homophobic place on earth. *Time.* https://content.time.com/time/world/article/0,8599,1182991,00.html

Powell, A., Davies, H. T. O., & Nutley, S. M. (2018). Facing the challenges of research-informed knowledge mobilization: 'Practising what we preach'? *Public Administration, 96*, 36–52. https://doi.org/10. 1111/padm.12365

Salazar, C. F. (2009). Strategies to survive and thrive in academia: The collective voices of counseling faculty of color. *International Journal od Advance Counselling, 31*, 181–198.

Sawyer, R. D., & Norris, J. (2013). *Duoethnography: Understanding qualitative research.* Oxford University Press.

Sawyer, R. D., & Norris, J. (2015). Hidden and null curricula of sexual orientation: A duoethnography of the absent presence and the present absence. *International Review of Qualitative Research, 8*(1), 5–26. https://doi.org/10.1525%2Firqr.2015.8.1.5

Scafidi, L. (2016). University history professor shines light on marginalization of black gay men through newly published book. *The Daily Illini.* https://dailyillini.com/news-stories/2016/04/03/university-history-professor-shines-light-on-marginalization-of-black-gay-men-through-newly-published-book/

Shetty, A. (2023). *Police believe gender-studies class targeted in University of Waterloo Stabbings of Associate Prof, 2 students.* CBC News. https://www.cbc.ca/news/canada/kitchener-waterloo/emergency-alert-university-waterloo-stabbing-wat-safe-1.6892506

Strayhorn, T. L., & Terrell, M. C. (Eds.). (2012). The evolving challenges of Black college students: New insights for policy, practice, and research. *Journal of College & University Student Housing, 38/39*(2/1), 140.

Sutton, J., & Tucker, E. (2023, June 29). *24-year-old suspect charged with stabbing 3 people during gender studies class at Canada's University of Waterloo in 'hate-motivated' attack, police say.* CNN. https://www.cnn.com/2023/06/29/americas/canada-waterloo-university-stabbing/index.html#:~:text=A%2024%2Dyear%2Dold%20student,%E2%80%9Chate%2Dmotivated%20incident.%E2%80%9D

Turner, C. S. V., Myers, S. L., & Creswell, J. W. (1999). Exploring underrepresentation: The case of faculty of color in the Midwest. *Journal of Higher Education, 70*(1), 1–21.

Van Dyke, N., & Tester, G. (2014). Dangerous climates: Factors associated with variation in racist hate crimes on college campuses. *Journal of Contemporary Criminal Justice, 30*(3), 290–309.

Verduzco-Baker, L. (2018). Modified brave spaces: Calling in *brave instructors. Sociology of Race and Ethnicity, 4*(4), 585–592.

Watson, K. R. (2023). *Navigating academic leadership hierarchy: Exploring Black male faculty members' advancement to senior-level leadership positions in Ontario universities* [Doctoral dissertation, University of Toronto]. ProQuest Dissertations Publishing.

VIGNETTE THREE

BLACK AND QUEER

I Belong!

Brandon Mack

The K–12 system always told me that Higher Education wasn't for someone like me. Black and Queer. Growing up, I was told that being smart meant that you were trying to be wWhite. My predominantly white K–12 education system told me that being Black and smart meant you were an exception, which made you a threat. When I was looking for higher education institutions, I was looking for a place that would allow me to be my fullest self, Black, Queer, and Smart. The institution I chose was predominantly White but had a diverse population, including support systems for Black students, so I was fortunate to find places and spaces in which I could have parts of myself supported. However, if I am truly honest, there were many times I was made aware that the institution wasn't created with me in mind. My place at the University would be questioned by my classmates, who assumed I was an athlete or that standards were lowered for my entry. When I used the LGBTQ+ resources, I would never see materials related to the intersections of being Black and Queer. I had to forge my place and space within my institution

The Journey: Truths of Same-Gender-Loving Black Males in Higher Education, pages 47–48.
Copyright © 2025 *Antione D. Tomlin*
Published under exclusive licence by Emerald Publishing Limited
ISBNs: 978-1-83708-498-2 HB, 978-1-83708-499-9 PB,
978-1-83708-500-2 EPDF, 978-1-83708-501-9 EPUB

that was benefiting from my Black brilliance. However, the question should be, why should it be so hard? The answer. It was designed to be, because I, and those like me, were not who higher education had in mind.

NARRATIVE FIVE

AM I BLACK AND GAY ENOUGH?

Richard Marks, Jr.

Being Black and gay has become more celebrated than in the past. Intersectionality is the vehicle for understanding the experiences of race, gender, sexual orientation, and other identities without apology. However, society often wants one to choose one identity to define oneself. The Black community continues to ostracize and shame those who identify as LGBTQIA, creating confusion, anger, and racial & cultural dissonance (Marks, 2015). While considerable strides have propelled "identity" as a main ingredient for humanity, as a black gay male administrator in higher education, I have to choose which identity is more salient, gay or Black. This chapter discusses some experiences as a Black, gay higher education administrator. Much more information is needed about the experiences of Black gay faculty and staff in higher education within the educational context. While black gay students' research is still limited but more accessible today, research on black and gay faculty and staff is nearly non-existence. Research is needed to hear the success and challenges Black gay faculty and staff experience as they have navigated the realm of higher education administration. We cannot help our students if, as administrators, we do not raise our voices to be heard.

Keywords: Black Gay Staff, Black Gay Administrator, Black Gay Faculty

The Journey: Truths of Same-Gender-Loving Black Males in Higher Education, pages 49–59.
Copyright © 2025 *Antione D. Tomlin*
Published under exclusive licence by Emerald Publishing Limited
ISBNs: 978-1-83708-498-2 HB, 978-1-83708-499-9 PB,
978-1-83708-500-2 EPDF, 978-1-83708-501-9 EPUB

In the last decade, there has been an increase in attention toward the LGBTQIA community. Visibility on screen and in music are a few examples of how our world has changed since the 90s. Policies, laws, and research have made positive strides in support of the LGBTQIA community. Yet, out of convenience, pop culture has continued to take up, appropriate, and profit from phrases and concepts like "shade" and "spilling tea," which emerged from poor and working-class Black queer, trans, and gender-nonconforming communities (Livingston, 1989; Lange et al., 2019). One would find this occurring in many career fields. History tells us that Black people have created, cooked, and seasoned most of what our white counterparts have taken for profit and gain. The taste most people enjoy has often been designed and prepared by Black or other people of color. Yet, the violence, disrespect, and discrimination among and within the LGBTQIA community, especially of color, continues to rise. Unfortunately, higher education is not without its struggle.

College is a place of exploration, discovery, and academic attainment. As first-year students, we were told to explore campus and discover ourselves by joining organizations, meeting new people, doing well academically, and graduating with as little debt as possible. The American dream is to go to college, get married, and have 2.5 children with a white picket fence and a car. Despite the social challenges of being Black and poor, I grew up believing this. I was going to be that Black man and make my family proud. Although I came from the lower-class projects in a major midwest city, I dreamed, like my white peers, that I, too, would be able to experience the American dream.

In the 90s, college experiences included clubs and organizations, fraternity parties, late-night studying, academics, relationships, and self-discoveries. As a young Black male at a large PWI in the midwest, I was immersed in my Black identity throughout college. Tichavakunda (2020) posits that despite the dominance of Whiteness on historically white campuses, Black students find moments and spaces to come together—sometimes only for hour-long meetings—and create Black places. My Blackness as a student was important, especially from a Black inner-city community and neighborhood.

As an undergrad, attending a PWI, the phenomenon around Black gayness centered around the term DL or "down low" and the military's campaign "Don't ask, don't tell." Interestingly, I found myself understanding the plight of the DL Brutha firsthand. Dating men and women, I took on the conquest of the hyper-sexual Black male, subscribing to the stereotypes to compensate for the hidden truth of my attraction to the same gender. Navigating my academics while growing more aware of my sexual preference, I became more comfortable accepting my gay identity. I secretly read books, E. Lynn Harris, my introductions to professional gay Black men, attempted online conversations, and attended a few gay clubs to help me understand my feelings. In addition, I desperately wanted to be in a community with others with other young, Black, and gay males. However, I continued to date women, but behind closed doors, my curiosity about dating men continued to grow. I wanted and needed the support of other Black gay men. For years, I secretly straddled the fence. It wasn't until I was working in my first professional position when I unequivocally abandoned the internal struggle to accept my gay identity. This feeling was freeing, especially in student affairs spaces. Participating in diversity workshops and listening to others tell their stories was part of the encouragement and support for why I was able to move into a space of acceptance among my professional peers in higher ed.

BEING GAY IN HIGHER EDUCATION

Colleges and universities have increasingly expanded their views on LGBTQ-IA students. While LGBTQIA organizations typically focus on the agenda and theories supporting the gay white male (Marks, 2015), researchers have brought awareness and education to the intersectionality of race, gender identity/expression, and belonging. For example, Strayhorn and Mullins (2012) conducted a qualitative study to understand the challenges that Black gay male undergraduates confront in campus residence halls and the supports that enabled their success. Mahoney's (2019) study analyzes a queer of color critique that centers around the queer of color subject and the social constructs of race, gender, sexuality, and class in cultural formations such as Black fraternities. Mobley discusses some challenges LGBT students encounter at HBCUs, resulting in recommendations to help HBCUs create a more affirming and inclusive campus environment for LGBT students. While higher education has expanded its view around LGBTQIA students, Black faculty and staff often find themselves closed in sharing their gay identity because of the cultural stigma among other Black professional peers, keeping personal business personal, and the challenge of being unable to progress professionally.

Higher education is one of the more accepting career fields that encourages you to be authentic. In my 20+ years of service in higher education, I have experienced gay professionals doing exceptional work in the field, especially those with an affinity for LGBTQIA students on campus. However, I do not see Black gay faculty and staff, specifically administrators, being as open about their gay identity amongst their peers and students. Being a Black gay male in higher education administration means I can openly express who I am partnered with without judgment, to some extent. Occasionally, I would catch some of my Black colleagues with their expressions that seemed to say, "Oh really, hmmm?" It is unfortunate when I feel I have to defend and explain myself to other Black people. As Black folk, we are our worst critics, which was a significant reason for the silence around my gay identity. Again, if asked about my sexuality, I choose to disclose or not to disclose. It is my business and mine alone. It is a privilege, not a right, to know my sexual identity and who I decide to spend quality time with. My experience with white professionals has been more accepting and embracing. Typically, I found their approach to be less intrusive and more supportive. Overall, being Black and gay in higher education has been welcoming.

EXPERIENCES THAT SHAPED MY JOURNEY
AS A BLACK GAY MALE IN HIGHER EDUCATION

As a new professional, I was more apprehensive about disclosing my gay identity to students and staff. I did not want the judgment. I was still determining who I could trust. And I was unsure and afraid of the backlash from my supervisors and other upper-level administrators who could easily prevent professional advancement. Reybold et al. (2008) share that professionals do not leave their personal beliefs and ethics behind when they begin the workday; they "bring their values with them" (Landau & Osmo, 2003, p. 42), and any application of ethical codes reflect those values. In other words, private and professional moralities are not separate spheres; both require "the investments of one's self" (Sorell, 1998, p. 22). Understanding that I must show up as myself, I had to learn and realize that my gay identity could not stay closeted if I were to be authentically me. It was up to me to navigate and negotiate my identities to advance and be accepted by my professional colleagues and the students I serve. The field of student affairs and higher education administration is small. And a strong reputation is essential. It's the perception others have of us, shaped by our actions and words that matter most. Yet, it's invisible and consequential. I did not want to risk my professional reputation on uncertain terms or conditions.

One of our governing bodies within the profession of student affairs is American College Personnel Association (ACPA). Every year, ACPA hosts a conference to support and foster college student learning for student affairs professionals and the higher education community. In the association, there were several standing committees. One of those standing committees was call the Standing Committee for Lesbian, Gay, and Bisexual Awareness (SCLGBA). The Standing Committee for Lesbian, Gay, and Bisexual Awareness would put on a drag show event to raise money for the committee and HIV/AIDS. Professionals from faculty, staff and graduate students would perform, in drag, to entertain and highlight the pride of being LGBTQIA. Conference attendees would come to this event demonstrating full support for the cause and their colleagues. The ACPA conference is where I experienced the open expression of gay professionals in higher education. It was overwhelming and refreshing all at once. It is one thing to see other white gay males expressing themselves freely, but to see other Black gay professionals who felt comfortable in their gay expression was exciting and encouraging. Moments like this were important because I felt it gave me a license to be me.

My experiences throughout the year at ACPA helped to shape my confidence in the field of higher education. I had never witnessed anyone expressing their sexuality in an open public forum at a professional event. While the expressions were mainly with white colleagues, the sprinkle of Black gay professionals was intriguing. The Black gay male professional remained reluctant to participate in the activities. Again, with the fear of exposure, I learned that other Black gay professionals held firm to the "DL" or "Don't ask, Don't tell" status. For years, I discovered other Black gay male professionals in higher education, but unspokenly, they steered clear of gay activities at conferences, at least in how they expressed themselves. In this vein, I found that "invite only" events, secret meetings to specific outings, and coded conversations became how Black gay males in higher education navigated who were gay in the field.

Navigating higher education as a Black gay male has been interesting. I have found myself in the company with some great Black gay male administrators in the profession where we can support each other in our journeys. Early in my career, I was able to connect with a season Black gay male administrator who has been one of the best mentors to me in this field. It was at an ACPA where I met this professional. His advice and guidance have been welcoming. I remember him specifically telling me to show up unequivocally and authentically myself. My identities are not an apology but an assurance of blessings to those who may share the same identities, find the courage to express their identities, and for those who admire my boldness and brilliance as an administrator. While the journey may feel alone in some instances, the network, though unspoken, has been encouraging as a Black gay male in higher education.

CHALLENGES AS A BLACK GAY MALE IN HIGHER EDUCATION

We encourage students to find mentors as they navigate their undergraduate careers. Identifying a mentor or role model to help guide and negotiate the higher education terrain has been touted as one of the most important supportive factors in ensuring the retention of students in colleges and universities (Bowser & Perkins, 1991; Patton & Harper, 2003; Sutton, 2006; Strayhorn & Terrell, 2023). With that said, it is not widely known how Black faculty and staff seek out mentorship, but when you add Black and gay to the equation, it can be even more complicated. Some institutions have been intentional about faculty of color mentorship. The struggle to attract and retain Black faculty and staff, especially at PWIs, is a concerning trend in higher education. Despite aspirations for diversity, the reality remains that underrepresented faculty need to be hired and retained in numbers sufficient to change the institution's demographics (Carlson & LaVenia, 2023).

My experience of finding other Black gay mentors in higher education has not been the most difficult because of my tenacity to ask and seek those relationships within the profession. However, the network within this demographic is small, selective, and private, sometimes on purpose. I can understand why other Black gay administrators may feel isolated and, in some ways, prefer to be. In my conversations with other Black gay administrators, the fear of others knowing their identity continues to plague the idea of negative exposure. As a result, the delay and fear of not advancing professionally, judgment, stereotyping, and isolation become part of the challenges some Black gay men face in this field. Some challenges of being a Black student at a PWI are compounded around access, retention, graduation rates, academic success, and belonging. Coupled with certain student demographics (first-generation, age, gender, race/ethnicity), college experiences (enrollment type, online learning, STEM major, college grades, living situation, Greek affiliation), and institutional characteristics (control type, minority-serving institution, selectivity, Carnegie type) may also play a role in this aspect of belongingness (Miller et al., 2019). If our students face these challenges, are our Black faculty and staff faced with similar challenges but on a professional level? I believe we are. While the status of students and professionals are different, being Black and gay, we continue to struggle similarly to the students we serve.

When we become a employee of an institution, there is an agreement to uphold the institution's mission, core values, and vision. Institutions are centered around their brand to attract faculty, staff, students, and other stakeholders to build a positive and sustaining legacy. How does the institution support Black gay administrators? Similar to our Black students, there is a lack of support for Black faculty and staff, and being gay is even of less importance. As a subpopulation of being Black, Black gay men not only face concerns similar to their heterosexual counterparts, but they also contend with the negative beliefs of others about homosexuality and intense homophobia in the Black community (Strayhorn, et al., 2008; Walls & Washington, 2006), Our sense of belonging as gay males within the Black community continues to be a struggle culturally, spiritually, and socially. Black college students, specifically at PWIs, continues to struggle with factors that impede their success, which contributes to the low retention and graduation rates (Haywood & Sewell, 2016). As a Black gay administrator in higher education, the institution's concern for me feels like a non-factor. Institutions give more lip service about their desire to increase and care for their faculty and staff of color, but I have yet to see true work in that effort. Similar to our Black gay male students in undergrad, we too face low retention and sense of belonging. Thus, more research about Black gay administrators would be helpful in breaking the silence.

Another challenge is isolation. Although I have established a network of Black gay men in the profession, I tend to be the only one of very few Black men at my workplace who identify as gay. For Black gay students at PWIs, research says that isolation was sometimes self-imposed as a way to prevent exposure of one's sexual orientation, while others had a hard time finding peers they could trust (Goode-Cross & Good, 2009; Patton, 2011; Roby, 2022). As a professional, I have experienced both connection and isolation as a means because of the disclosure of my sexual identity. Some of the responses and interactions I receive and perceive from my Black colleagues sometimes make me feel like I am not equal or less than others because of my sexual identity. While no one has ever said anything derogatory or inflammatory to me, the sense I sometimes feel encourages me to isolate myself to avoid what I assume to be judgment and backhand criticism. The number of Black faculty and staff is typically small at PWIs. It is disheartening to feel like you do not belong, intentionally or unintentionally.

For this reason, I believe this challenge in higher education continues to breed the unspoken treatment and intentional silence among Black gay higher education administrators. I was often alone and, to some extent, understood why one chooses to isolate themselves. In this instance, my Blackness, my most salient identity, is how I navigated my higher education administration spaces. It seems to be less complicated. While I do not seem to get resistance from my white professional counterparts, my Black professional peers give me pause. Much of this derives from the impediments stemming from the cultural dissonance and stereotypes around Black identity.

REWARDS AS A BLACK GAY ADMINISTRATOR

Diversity, equity, inclusion, and belonging are rising in colleges and universities, despite some state governments fighting diversity, critical race theory, and teaching oppression and discrimination in United States history. Diversity initiatives are an integral part of most organizations. As a Black gay administrator, it has been rewarding to be a practitioner in diversity. But there is still a long way to go. While student bodies may be increasingly representative of the growing diversity of our broader communities, work must be done with intentionality to diversity to change academic leadership, too. Students want to see that their school leaders are people they can relate to—and who have their interests in mind.

As a Black gay administrator, it is rewarding when students see me as a role model because of my identity. This sense of belonging encourages them in their navigation and experiences as a student at the institution. Belonging is the sense of feeling accepted and valued. It is the desire to have a sense of purpose at work and a sense of community (West, 2022). Garofalo (2019) posits, "Diversity is a fact, inclusion is a behavior, but belonging is an emotional outcome that people want in their organizations" (McGregor, 2019; West, 2022). As other studies found, the Black gay men felt being mentored by peers, faculty, and staff with whom they felt comfortable disclosing their sexual orientation helped them to have a deep commitment to the institution and their persistence in their endeavors (Goode-Cross & Tager, 2011; Marks, 2015). The reward is knowing that students who trust me by disclosing their sexual identity; perceive me as a role model, bring support, and affirm why I became a student affairs practitioner.

One would think that higher education would avoid stereotyping and discrimination. As human beings, regardless of career, stereotypes exist. Unfortunately, higher education is not without fault. As a Black man, I have fought against negative stereotypes my entire life. At school, work, and in public, the Black male is negatively portrayed in society as angry, lazy, uneducated, worthless, untrustworthy, and violent. While some hold on to the negative portrayal of Black men through media and historical reference, I have found some reward in the messaging and interactions from my white colleagues when they learn of my gay identity. I found it fascinating. While I would not say it was a reward, I would call it more of a benefit. My observation with my white counterparts around my gay identity seems minimize or eliminate the guard we typically feel. In my experience, I have found their engagement to be more pleasant, easier to talk to, and more readily to assist me in the workplace.

In my experience, white female colleagues seem to feel more comfortable in their approach to me. It is not spoken but feels different, especially when another Black male is assumed to be straight. While professional decorum occurs in all interactions, I have felt more favored and liked than the other Black and assumed to be straight males. For example, I and another Black male colleague had to report to our supervisor some information regarding an issue within the department. The Black male colleague, who is typically met with some resistance, is questioned more accusingly. Being a team player, I took the lead to deliver the information to our supervisor. While we both worked to resolve the situation, it was obvious how she was more than receptive hearing from me than my other Black male colleague. While I cannot be sure if it was my gay identity that allowed me to benefit from my white female colleagues favor. I believe women of all races tend to feel more relaxed because of my gay identity, dispelling some of the negative stereotypes typically associated with Black males.

BEING AUTHENTIC IN HIGHER EDUCATION

Higher education is a place for self-discovery and reinvention. Through self-discovery, students learn how to describe themselves in more dimensions than merely their grades and position in the class. The focus should be on increasing each student's capacity to be self-reflective. As an administrator, I learned to be my full and authentic self through the experiences I have had in my life, especially in my career. My dedication as a higher education administrator in student affairs provides a powerful legacy I leave with the students and community I serve. Speaking with other Black gay professionals in other careers, higher education leaves room for one to be authentically and unequivocally who you are and want to be. This freedom of expression is on multiple levels. Your authentic self is who you are deep down. The part of you that doesn't care what others think.

I show up every day as myself without apology. However, time and place are necessary for one's navigation in this field. I have navigated spaces without making others uncomfortable, challenging their negative assumptions, and providing opportunities for dialogue and critical thought. I did not always feel this confident in my expression and disclosure of my gay identity, but I have found support in other fellow Black gay colleagues, both in and out of the field of higher education. Additionally, I am excited about contributing to more research about Black gay administrators and the parallel to the Black gay student. In concert with our national associations in student affairs and many other professional associations, the encouragement to be free in all of who you are is essential to the fabric of higher learning.

STRATEGIES TO SUPPORT BLACK GAY ADMINISTRATORS

Research suggests many recommendations to support Black gay students at PWIs. Patton (2011) indicates that mentoring and role-modeling, to which Washington and Wall (2006) referred, can be an excellent resource for Black gay male students. Goode-Cross and Tager (2011) posit that future studies may also broaden the focus to include the roles of gender and social class in students' experiences. Another recommendation is for faculty and staff to participate in, connect with, and take away something from diversity training (Handy, 2017). Similarly, I think there are some strategies that Black gay higher education administrators should note, including in their navigation in higher education.

Mentorship and role modeling are certainly a strategy that has served me well in my journey as a practitioner. Generally speaking, being mentored by peers, faculty, and staff with those who share your identity can be helpful. This connection, specifically at PWIs, deepens one's commitment to the institution and sense of belonging. Attending professional conferences, participating on committees focused on gay support for faculty, staff, and students, and lending your valued experience to other Black gay administrators are ways in which Black gay male administrators can help young Black gay college students. It will take you being open and comfortable to do so. Understanding that trust can be a concern, allow yourself some grace to share your story with others. You will find more positive results as other professionals will also be likely to share.

Another tip would be to attend Black faculty and staff outings. As discussed earlier, trust can be a factor in disclosing one's sexual identity. Participating in these events and activities would allow you to observe and create a space to build relationships and discover others with the same identity. Also, since Black faculty and staff demographics are already small, I would expand efforts to include other LGBTQIA of color. Building relationships within this community can be an excellent remedy, eliminating some feelings of isolation.

Lastly, higher education can only do so much. It is crucial to expand outside the higher education field to establish a healthy and supportive community. I have found those who I have friended as professional Black gay males have been an added ingredient to my experience professionally and personally. Since there are limitations in finding those like-minded individuals in higher education, their shared experiences can also be of great support. Research needs to extend to our Black gay faculty and staff. The data would benefit the academy and serve as a resource for higher education to address not only the concerns of our students but those of us who serve them as well.

REFERENCES

Bowser, B. P., & Perkins, H. W. (1991). *Mentoring: An effective tool for the retention of minorities*. ERIC Clearinghouse. https://eric.ed.gov/?id=ED342841

Carlson, J. A., & LaVenia, K. N. (2023). The importance of transformational leadership to support faculty diversity in our nation's predominantly white institutions of higher learning. *Journal of Cases in Educational Leadership, 26*(1), 71–81.

Garofalo, L. A. (2019). Diversity, inclusion, and belonging in higher education: Understanding the emotional dimensions of student engagement. *Journal of Higher Edu-*

cation Policy and Management, 41(2), 118–130. https://doi.org/10.1080/136008
0X.2019.1581301

Goode-Cross, R., & Good, G. E. (2009). Black gay students at predominantly white institutions: The intersection of race, sexuality, and isolation. *Journal of Black Psychology, 35*(4), 475–496. https://doi.org/10.1177/0095798409334982

Goode-Cross, D. T., & Tager, D. (2011). Negotiating multiple identities: How African-American gay and bisexual men persist at a predominantly White institution. *Journal of Homosexuality, 58*(9), 1235–1254.

Handy, J. L. (2017). *Black & gay today: Experiences with perceived racial and sexual orientation microaggressions in predominately white colleges and universities* (Doctoral dissertation). The Chicago School of Professional Psychology.

Haywood, J. L., Jr., & Sewell, S. (2016). Against all odds: Implications for low income African American male students seeking a college degree at a predominately white college. *Race, Gender & Class, 23*(3–4), 109–128.

Landau, R., & Osmo, R. (2003). Professional and personal hierarchies of ethical principles. *International Journal of Social Welfare, 12*(1), 42–49.

Lange, A. C., Duran, A., & Jackson, R. (2019). The state of LGBT and queer research in higher education revisited: Current academic houses and future possibilities. *Journal of College Student Development, 60*(5), 511–526.

Livingston, J. (Director). (1990). *Paris is burning* [Film]. Off White Productions.

Logan, S. R., & Dudley, H. S. (2021). The "double-whammy" of being Black and a woman in higher education leadership. In S. R. Logan & H. S. Dudley (Eds.), *Research anthology on instilling social justice in the classroom* (pp. 1545–1565). IGI Global.

Mahoney, A. D. (2019). *Queering Black Greek-lettered fraternities, masculinity and manhood: A queer of color critique of institutionality in higher education.* Electronic Theses and Dissertations. Paper 3286. https://doi.org/10.18297/etd/3286

Marks, R. B. (2015). *As the world turns: Being black and gay on campus in the 21st century.* University of Southern California.

McGregor, J. (2019). Diversity, inclusion, and belonging: Understanding the emotional impacts on organizational culture. *Organizational Psychology Review, 9*(3), 179–191. https://doi.org/10.1177/2041386619850145

Miller, A. L., Williams, L. M., & Silberstein, S. M. (2019). Found my place: The importance of faculty relationships for seniors' sense of belonging. *Higher Education Research & Development, 38*(3), 594–608.

Mobley, S. D., Jr., & Johnson, J. M. (2015). The role of HBCUs in addressing the unique needs of LGBT students. *New Directions for Higher Education, 2015*(170), 79–89.

Patton, L. D. (2011). Perspectives on identity, disclosure, and the campus environment among African American gay and bisexual men at one historically Black college. *Journal of College Student Development, 52*(1), 77–100.

Patton, L. D., & Harper, S. R. (2003). Mentoring relationships among African American women in graduate and professional schools. *New Directions for Student Services, 104,* 67–78. https://doi.org/10.1002/ss.108

Reybold, L. E., Halx, M. D., & Jimenez, A. L. (2008). Professional integrity in higher education: A study of administrative staff ethics in student affairs. *Journal of College Student Development 49*(2), 110–124. doi:10.1353/csd.2008.0013

Roby, S. (2022). *Narratives of agency: LGBTQ+ African American students thriving at a predominantly white institution.* Southern Illinois University at Carbondale.

Sorell, T. (1998). Beyond the fringe? The strange state of business ethics. In M. Parker (Ed.), *Ethics & organizations* (pp. 15–29). Sage.

Strayhorn, T. L., Blakewood, A. M., & DeVita, J. M. (2008). Factors affecting the college choice of African American gay male undergraduates: Implications for retention. *National Association of Student Affairs Professionals Journal, 11*(1), 88–108.

Strayhorn, T. L., & Mullins, T. G. (2012). Investigating Black gay male undergraduates' experiences in campus residence halls. *Journal of College & University Student Housing, 38*(2), 70–82. https://www.ncsu.edu/journal-of-college-and-university-student-housing

Sutton, E. M. (2006). Developmental mentoring of college students: A viable retention strategy for students of color. *NASPA Journal, 43*(4), 613–631. https://doi.org/10.2202/0027-6014.1746

Strayhorn, T. L., & Terrell, M. C. (Eds.). (2023). *The evolving challenges of Black college students: New insights for policy, practice, and research.* Taylor & Francis.

Tichavakunda, A. A. (2020). Studying Black student life on campus: Toward a theory of Black placemaking in higher education. *Urban Education*, 0042085920971354.

Walls, N. E., & Washington, T. A. (2006). The role of race, class, and sexual identity in the mental health of Black gay and bisexual men. *American Journal of Public Health, 96*(9), 1673–1676. https://doi.org/10.2105/AJPH.2005.078057

Washington, D. C., & Wall, L. T. (2006). The role of mentorship for Black gay male students at predominantly white institutions. *Journal of Black Gay Studies, 14*(2), 204–220. https://doi.org/10.1080/19321682.2006.10379507

West, C. (2022). Diversity, equity, inclusion, belonging, and antiracism. In *Fast facts about diversity, equity, and inclusion in nursing: Building competencies for an antiracism practice* (p. 97). Springer Publishing. https://doi.org/10.1891/9780826165284.0030

NARRATIVE SIX

HEY CIS!

Sean Rice Jr.

This chapter will highlight the power of understanding intersectionality and ally-ship on my personal journey to living unapologetically in both my Queerness & Blackness in higher education which later became my profession. Growing up, as young Black men, elders tell us to walk with our heads held high, but who is tilting the heads of Black queer folks, as we are dehumanized because of our sexuality? I will discuss how my relationships with cis heterosexuals and active allies empowered me to self-awareness and self-authorship. The key word was "active" and comprehending that "ally" is a verb, not a noun. I will talk about the importance of friendship and the development of relationships with others and the most important relationship, with the "man in the mirror".

Keywords: Intersectionality, Allyship, Cis-gendered, Self-Authorship

IN THE BEGINNING

Hey cis! I am talking to you. Yes, you! It is time for us to come together. As a same gender loving (SGL) Black man in higher education, I understand the power of education and working toward a common goal! Our goal needs to be to lead with love and respect as we work for the advancement of the Black com-

The Journey: Truths of Same-Gender-Loving Black Males in Higher Education, pages 61–67.
Copyright © 2025 *Antione D. Tomlin*
Published under exclusive licence by Emerald Publishing Limited
ISBNs: 978-1-83708-498-2 HB, 978-1-83708-499-9 PB,
978-1-83708-500-2 EPDF, 978-1-83708-501-9 EPUB

munity collectively. I apologize for giving you a directive without building any rapport or introducing myself. Again, Hey Cis! "Cisgender, or simply cis, is an adjective that describes a person whose gender identity aligns with the sex they were assigned at birth" (Wamsley, 2021). I am a Black cis-gay man, that is also a hopeful romantic seeking a shot at the American Dream with another man. Which means I have experienced unlearning the negative viewpoint that society forced upon me to be ashamed of who I am. I had to build myself up with a foundation of self-love. I previously navigated spaces, with my heart in my hands ready to give it to anyone that needed it, to in return be ridiculed for challenging the concept of what a man should be through my expression. To be a same-gender-loving Black man in higher education, is to be present and triumphant in the daily battles of our existence. We must be confident in how we show up as our livelihood is denied and invalidated regularly. It is a challenge to be a hopeful romantic that loves, love and to be the representation for demographics that society believes to not value education. To be a Black SGL Man on campus is to be a mentor for Black male students and queer students. It is critical to share our stories unapologetically to safeguard the generations after us from the obstacles we once faced.

To be told you are too much, you're extra, and that I was gay before I could claim the sexual orientation for myself, shows the need for positive role models in developmental spaces. It is a plus for cis-het individuals to understand and empathize with us, but to share experiences and have space to share your stories that could potentially save someone from making the same mistakes is another level of care and understanding. That level of care allowed me to establish my passion in the field of student affairs.

STUDENT AFFAIRS PROFESSIONAL

My undergraduate story was a tale of a naive boy, attempting to show the world I was an adult while enduring a toxic relationship and attempting to achieve success academically. I was highly involved on campus and received life changing mentorship and guidance from student affairs professionals. If I did not encounter these professionals, I would not be the person, nor the professional I am today. These individuals first saw my potential and then saw that extra spark that was my queerness. They did not direct me to tone down that spark, they created space for me to lead with my queerness and respected me for who I am. These professionals facilitated one on one sessions, shared involvement opportunities and gave me permission to show-up authentically. I want to pay forward the same impact these professionals made on my journey.

As a student affairs professional on a college campus, my goal is to support students on their college journeys in and outside the classroom. We focus on supporting students holistically in understanding that there will be several hurdles along the way. I recognize that I could connect with all students but there's a special connection in working with marginalized students who share intersecting identities. While I want this chapter to celebrate the relationships between SGL men and heterosexual people, I wouldn't be me without addressing some of the challenges we face while bridging the gaps between the communities. It starts with mutual respect. Once an individual comes out, they must first sit with the possibility of being isolated or even estranged from their families and friends because of who they love, so mutual grace is crucial in these relationships.

THE MOUNTAIN

A story or concept is rarely shared without conflict and drama along the way. Some of my challenges in being my proud Black SGL self in higher education have been the invalidation of my queerness in man dominated spaces such as barbershops and sport bars. Also, for individuals to hide behind their religion to spew hate toward me outside of queer spaces. There was also conflict with acceptance from family members and to accept my identity for myself. One of the hardest challenges is the compacted labor of our identities, students that identify with us, come to our office for everything and because we can be at times the only professional they resonate with take on the challenge. We are also usually tapped to support entire student populations without consideration of how our marginalized identities bring a great deal of emotional and physical labor based in doing DEI work without additional compensation.

PRIDE

Although I've experienced challenges along the way, I have experienced some rewards standing in my primary identities, such as seeing the value in our collective power. Once we come together, it is like a Megazord preparing for a battle in full force. The talents of Black people are often considered magic and Black gay men have a little extra razzle dazzle in our talents and passions. Another reward has been acknowledging that our current student populations are the future and knowing that we have a part in supporting the next generation. As our Black ancestors had to create their own lanes during the Civil Rights Movement, we are creating FUBU (For us by us) spaces for Black gay men to foster our relationships and gifts. These rewards help in developing our melanated pride.

SELF-AUTHORSHIP

Self-authorship was a developmental theory that was presented in my grad program. "'Self-Authorship is the capacity to internally define a coherent belief system and identity that coordinates mutual relations with others.' Baxter Magnolia, Professor of Educational Leadership at Miami University" (Le Cunff, 2002). This theory defines the process of bringing my full authentic self to higher education spaces. If I existed as my authentic self, I would not construct how I show-up, I would take every step that I am meant to take on my journey despite naysayers.

Other ways I show up unapologetically in my Blackness and Queerness are using dialect/terms from my primary identity groups daily. Also, by having the freedom to wear what I want and what is comfortable for me. Then to share my weekend or outside of work experiences and authentically be asked about my experiences with follow-up conversations.

NOT SO SORRY FOR THE BLINDING LIGHT

As previously discussed, Black SGL men need active allies, and I would like to share some tips to build authentic relationships and ways to affirm these beautiful Black men which will allow them space to fly above the negativity and toward greatness. A growth mindset is essential in creating space for us to grow together. Always be a sponge or life-learner when it comes to understanding Black gay men in higher education. Language and terms are ever-evolving and when you close the institution or yourself off from learning, you are doing your colleagues and your intuition a disservice by invalidating the experiences and existence of gay men.

Black Gay men live for our Black Queens with our full chest and when it is time for Black women to challenge their peers or partners in their homophobia or support us against the hatred that is flooding pop culture, the room goes silent. So, show-up for us (gay men) as we show up for everyone else. Recognize our contribution to the community and culture. Allow us to tell our stories and contribute to community conversations and progression by intentionally creating space or making room for our stories and obstacles. Lastly, do your self-work and practice self-love because when your foundation is set, you have more capacity to spread love and be open to love! RuPaul Charles said it best, "If you can't love yourself, how in the hell are you going to love somebody else" (Charles, *Host* 2009)?

DON'T CALL YOU CIS?

There have been multiple articles and celebrities in an uproar about the use of the identifing term cis-gender. This scientific term is not slang that the LGBTQIA+ community came up with to be derogatory toward our straight counterparts. This identify term is address the distention between transgender folks. There has also been pushback on the use of preferred names and pronouns. To experience inequality in this form is a double slap in the face for Black Queer individuals. We just want to coexist and thrive.

MEETING AT THE CORNER OF BLACK & GAY

I am unable to discuss my journey in higher education without addressing the concept of intersectionality, which was coined by a Black woman, Kimberlé Crenshaw, in 1989. "The concept of intersectionality describes the ways in which systems of inequality based on gender, race, ethnicity, sexual orientation, gender identity, disability, class and other forms of discrimination "intersect" to create unique dynamics and effects" (Center for Intersectional Justice, 2023). I define it as the identity load that we carry in the world. Standing strong in my Blackness is challenging every day and then to add my queerness load and being a first-generation college student makes the identities that I carry heavier in the fight toward success in academia. I have always heard the saying that you need to crawl before you can walk, but it is rare that the load that you are carrying is taken into consideration along your journey to walking in all that you are.

DEI PROFESSIONAL

Coming into the field of student affairs, my why was to support marginalized students that were seeking to find their sense of belonging and their support person on campus. All my internships and practicums were focused on Diversity, Equity, & Inclusion functional areas. After having a unique experience in housing, I found my way to upstate New York to run a diversity center! In this role, I was able to support marginalized students in multiple forms. This experience let me know I was making an impact in how students would want to just come into the space I created, want advice, and were vulnerable sharing their stories.

I also answered the call to co-chair the LGBTQIA+ employee resource group that also served the institution in programing. In this role, I was able to unpack generational trauma and expand my knowledge about identity. I was able to see individuals that did not identify with the community but were actively learning about the queer community. They were trained in our version of Safe Zone and began to train their peers. These allies showed up for more than the pride celebrations. Their openness to learn and grow was a catalyst in this role which affirmed to me that I was in control of my destiny and the power that I have in my identities.

THE WEB OF CLUBHOUSE

An experience that helped shape my identity as a Black, same-gender-loving male was during the height of the pandemic and quarantining. At that time, everyone was stuck inside, while also seeking community outside of our own mind. I was able to find and curate a space on the audio app, "Clubhouse." I came together with a group of talented Black Queer men to create the group, "Black Gay Men Chat"! On the app, we were able to highlight the lived experiences of Black SGL men across the world. I tapped into my creativity and my " and in so many ways, by producing multiple projects such as: a talent show through the "Black & Gay" group, a seductive improv audio show, "The Art of Seduction", a shoot your shot show "The Black Gay Bachelor", a book club called "Reading Rainbow", and facilitating/moderating multiple conversations across the platform (crystal meth in the Black Queer community, Black Gay Fatherhood, Dating Red Flags, etc.). This experience shaped my identity because I was able to share/facilitate a space with individuals that were able to challenge and validate my lived experiences, while bringing new perspectives to the conversations. Our group currently has 7,000+ members and showed me the power and influence that we have as Black Queer people. I recognize that at times society will not accept us fully which was evident in heterosexual spaces on the app where the expectation was for us to show-up

Black first, without regard for the idea that we are full people, and we deserve to share and take up all the space we can as such.

COHORT EXPERIENCE

A time when my identity was challenged and my foundation of self-awareness was developed, was when I returned to school to pursue my master's degree, a Master of Science in college student affairs with a concentration in conflict resolution and analysis. Part of my program was highly focused on supporting students holistically and understanding values and finding your "why". The most impactful part of my grad journey was that my program was cohort-based. I embarked on this journey with twenty-eight diverse individuals, that I attended classes with, lived in the same graduate apartment building, and collaborated in our assistantships across campus functional areas.

Our program was intentional in our personal and professional development and the stage was set with an enlightening exercise that was presented during our orientation. When facilitating this exercise there were identities listed around the room, identities such as: race, gender, sexual orientation, religion, education, etc. Then the facilitator asked questions like, which identity do you feel you are judged for the most? Which is your primary identity? Which identity brings you the most conflict? Once the question is asked, participants moved under the identity that matched their answer and then were asked to share. I felt the facilitator and this exercise empowered me to come out and lead with my SGL identity for the first time. As someone who was outed, I feel a need to safeguard who I shared my queerness with.

From this exercise, I was upfront about who I was and how I showed-up in this program and socially. I was able to build authentic relationships with colleagues from diverse backgrounds, which have shaped me into the person and professional that I am today. I built one relationship with a cis-heterosexual Black man almost instantly as we were paired to be roommates during the graduate assistantship interview weekend. Our friendship was refreshing and showed me that outside of my line brothers in my fraternity and my actual brothers, true brotherhood is possible between gay and straight men. An indication that our relationship was real was him actually asking about my dating experiences and creating space for me to share stories that centered my queerness.

Socially, I would go to multiple clubs with my cohort members, we went to school in south Florida, so the nightlife was like a forever spring break and majority of the establishments we frequented were straight establishments. I was always able to have fun, but it was rare for us to go to gay establishments. I was able to build community with the other queer cohort members and we were able to find the gayborhood! My focus was usually for us to enjoy ourselves and be comfortable, centering the needs of the whole group. However, for my birthday, I gave myself permission to center my needs and interests, I planned a whole weekend of events. Friday: dinner and karaoke, Saturday: art Basel, happy hour and night out in the gayborhood, and Sunday: brunch! Yes, I'm extra. I was so thankful to have a group of 20 people come out for dinner to celebrate me, the karaoke establishment was a gay dive bar and I pre-warned everyone of that, and everyone was fine to get to the next venue! As we entered the establishment, there was pornography on all the TVs, and it was interesting to observe everyone's reactions to the space. There was awareness, discomfort, and confusion. It was intriguing for my straight counterparts to experience the feelings that I experience in their spaces often.

At the end of the night everyone was able to enjoy themselves and create a memory that they would never forget. I was thankful for them being open to experiencing our spaces. They have returned to queer spaces and ask questions. I have friends and associates that have never asked to go with me into gay spaces and never shared interest of my experiences outside of our relationship.

For us to evolve and come together there must be acknowledgement, openness, and humanization of our experiences. Life is too short for queer folks to dim their lights for others' comfort. We are whole people, and we cannot strip ourselves of part of who we are to be palpable or for you to allow us to have a seat at the table. So, I say again "Hey cis"! Not as a shady greeting, but as an invitation to be open, be loving, and to be a true ally.

A LETTER FROM MY CIS BRO

Hey bro,

I hope you're doing well. Being the minority in higher education, I've had quite the time for reflection. The privilege I've been carrying is important to acknowledge as it relates to the burden you've had to lug around. I'm here to remind you that I will see you, I appreciate you and I'm with you. For progress to be achieved, I must ensure I know how to show up for you. I have taken the initiative to be Safe Space trained and become a Safe Space facilitator. It's imperative to do the work to educate others, it shouldn't fall on you. I'm committed to sustaining my allyship until the end of time. There's no reason why I can't co-exist with you. I'm optimistic one day the rest of world will follow suit. Until then, I will continue to have your back and stick up for you especially when I'm in rooms without you.

I'm not perfect nor are my other cis', but please extend grace as mistakes will occur. There's a revolving door and a new crop that has to be educated around the clock. Don't hesitate to check me if I'm ever wrong or incorrect. I find a lot of value in adding foundation to our bridge of worlds because we are stronger together than apart. Our field may feel free for you to be yourself, but that's not the case for everyone. I plan to be persistent in cultivating space for you to simply be yourself and not let anyone or anything ostracize you more than society already does. Please let me know how else I can push my allyship further.

Love,

Cis (Cedric Blatch, M.S.)

VIGNETTE FOUR

PROTECTING MY SAME-GENDER LOVINGNESS AND PEACE

Rodrick Johnson

I was determined to prove that not only was I same gender loving that I was an expert in my field, I was that college professor she wanted to be, but I was also firm and fair…then I met him! Here I was teaching my poor little heart out, and to protect his name, I will call him Ken. Ken was an intelligent kid, and when I say kid, he was about 19, so in my mind, I still viewed him as a kid, but in his mind, he viewed us as equal. Ken was so fascinated by the way I was able to communicate content, how I was able to swiftly give everyone feedback, how I was able to support the class environment and make sure that they had everything that they needed to be successful in each assignment. The problem with Ken is that Ken knew what he was supposed to do, but he felt as though he did not have to rise to the occasion because he was flirtatious. Once I realized what Ken was doing, I started to take note of his interactions with me, and I noticed that his interactions were not respectful. I am not saying he was disrespectful, but it was not

The Journey: Truths of Same-Gender-Loving Black Males in Higher Education, pages 69–70.
Copyright © 2025 *Antione D. Tomlin*
Published under exclusive licence by Emerald Publishing Limited
ISBNs: 978-1-83708-498-2 HB, 978-1-83708-499-9 PB,
978-1-83708-500-2 EPDF, 978-1-83708-501-9 EPUB

respectful as a college professor and a student; it was more relational. It was more that he wanted something more profound than I could not give him. Being a part of the same gender-loving community, sometimes manipulation is done without you knowing. When I caught wind of the manipulation and understood what he wanted, I started to move differently.

NARRATIVE SEVEN

IN AUTHENTICITY

(De)Valuing Same-Gender-Loving "BlaQueer" Men in Higher Education

David Sterling Brown

Building on Dr. T. Anansi Wilson's "BlaQueer" concept that recognizes the dual status of being openly Black and queer, this essay challenges higher education institutions to recognize the dangers of not protecting the vulnerable Black and queer population. One way the essay does this is by questioning DEI and anti-racist agendas that can, at times, still be anti-Black and homophobic in practice. While simultaneously acknowledging the rewards of a BlaQueer positionality in higher education, Brown discloses personal-experiential anecdotes that touch on forms of sexual violence in a critically engaged way. Brown also critiques the usage of "safe space" rhetoric and argues that higher education institutions should instead adopt and promote a "productive discomfort" philosophy that recognizes the impossibility of everyone being, or feeling, safe in any given moment.

Keywords: BlaQueer, Racial Whiteness, Injustice, Authenticity, White Supremacy, Equity, Survival, Silence, Critical-Personal-Experiential, Shakespeare, Hamlet, Violence, Intersectionality

The Journey: Truths of Same-Gender-Loving Black Males in Higher Education, pages 71–81.
Copyright © 2025 *Antione D. Tomlin*
Published under exclusive licence by Emerald Publishing Limited
ISBNs: 978-1-83708-498-2 HB, 978-1-83708-499-9 PB,
978-1-83708-500-2 EPDF, 978-1-83708-501-9 EPUB

If "to be Black and an intellectual in America is to live in a box, not of my own making, and on the box is a label not of my own choosing," then what is it to be Black and an intellectual who is same-gender-loving (Carter, 1991, 1)? More specifically, what is it to be a "BlaQueer" man whose distinctive presence in the so-called ivory tower threatens (Wilson, 2017, para. 7)—for some folk, or perhaps many, given the academy's high percentage of non-Black employees—"the dominator imperialist white supremacist capitalist patriarchal culture" that formed higher education's foundation, especially in the United States (hooks 2015, ix)? I understand that "most of those who have not met me, and many of those who have, see the box and read the label and imagine they have seen me" (Carter, 1991, 1). But, they have not seen me. They do not see me because they have been conditioned and socialized to see only a perception of me that exists within the DuBoisian "Veil" (Du Bois, 2011, p. 1; Jones, 2005). Given this reality, I often seek reassurance from the central message in Langston Hughes' poem "Mother to Son," which offers some answers to the questions above and even helps me regain my footing when I lose sight of my purpose, when the challenges seem like too much to bear:

Well, son, I'll tell you:
Life for me ain't been no crystal stair.
It's had tacks in it,
And splinters,
And boards torn up,
And places with no carpet on the floor—
Bare.
But all the time
I'se been a-climbin' on,
And reachin' landin's,
And turnin' corners,
And sometimes goin' in the dark
Where there ain't been no light.
So boy, don't you turn back.
Don't you set down on the steps
'Cause you finds it's kinder hard.
Don't you fall now—
For I'se still goin', honey,
I'se still climbin',
And life for me ain't been no crystal stair. (Hughes, 1994)

Due to my amplified awareness of social injustices and the mechanisms keeping them alive, life in higher education has meant experiencing an increase in exposure to the racism- and homophobia-related challenges from which I naively thought earning a PhD would liberate me. Life in higher education has meant securing my dream of being a tenured college professor by defining, and then re-defining, what I am striving for in my career. And life in the ivory tower has meant recognizing that nothing about occupying space in a place not built for me will be easy, nothing—one can only make it look so. But it never is. And yet, despite the struggle being all too real, I press on, we BlaQueer men climb on.

In authenticity—that is to say, in showing up daily as our authentic selves—we dare to climb on because we know the costs of inauthenticity. Either we were taught early on to be ourselves unapologetically; or we learned through experience, what I consider the hard way. We BlaQueer men remove from the box those labels not of our own choosing, replacing them with our own identifiers that remind us to live in authenticity. For the costs of *not* doing so, the costs for "turn[ing] back" or "sitting down" or "fall[ing]" to the ground and staying there are too high (Hughes, 2002). Removing the labels imposed on us by society, we free ourselves to an extent by rejecting pervasive assumptions about who we are. We free ourselves and step outside of the box and into our own. Despite the potential dangers of stepping out—dangers that could lead to us become targets of anti-BlaQueerness or become ostracized professionally or suffer on the mental health front—we free ourselves to express, and be, ourselves on our own terms because we know that inauthenticity, like our silence, will not protect us (Lorde, 2017).[1]

OUTSIDE THE BOX: (RE)SHAPING THE SELF

For same-gender-loving Black men, understanding that higher education institutions are part of, and not apart from, the world requires recognizing the dangers of inauthenticity. This is key to our survival. Such understanding also requires us to confront and accept, but not tolerate, the contradictory truth that institutions, and the people within them, can and *do* value and devalue us at the same time—and they have for centuries. Now that I have nearly a decade of experience in higher education, not including my New York University graduate school years and my Trinity College Ann Plato predoctoral fellowship year, I am convinced that authenticity is our primary mode of protection even as it paradoxically renders us more visible and therefore more vulnerable.

Authenticity is our strength (Wiest, 2020, 202).[2] It is the life-support system that keeps us going when life gets "kinder hard" (Hughes, 2002). It keeps us going, keeps us striving, because the engine of authenticity is our grit and integrity. One cannot truly have the latter with an inauthentic sense of self. I know this now. I learned the hard way because I entered higher education—that is, I began graduate school at New York University—without a clear sense of self on both personal and professional levels. About seven months before I started grad school, I had just revealed to my family that I am gay, at age 25. I was in an incredibly vulnerable and volatile place in my life, to say the least, while healing then physically,

---

[1] Lorde, Audre (2017). *Your Silence Will Not Protect You*. Silver Press.
[2] Wiest, Brianna (2020). *The Mountain Is You: Transforming Self-Sabotage Into Self-Mastery*. Thought Catalog Books.

psychologically and emotionally from a domestic violence incident that occurred about a week before my first term at NYU began. I almost didn't make it.

One early experience that shaped who I am as a Black same-gender-loving male in higher education occurred at the first grad school reception I went to at my program's start. I recall now the sheer excitement I felt about what I was doing in that space and what that space would do for me, personally and professionally. As I navigated the reception room and engaged with my new cohort mates, I eventually had a conversation with a white woman grad student who could see I was Black and soon learned I was gay when I mentioned I would be commuting to NYC from Connecticut, where I lived with my then partner. Without missing a beat, upon learning I am a same-gender-loving Black man, personal information that was not easy to convey after telling my family only a few months before, this white woman said, "Black and gay, you must have checked *all* the boxes." Dear Reader: Sit with those words now, knowing I *had* to do so back then because I was not yet in the place I am today where ignorance gets returned to sender, immediately. My rose-colored glasses got damaged at that Fall 2009 reception. And so, I eventually took them off.

Stunned by this white woman's insensitivity, her audaciously offensive insult, I felt myself shrink, yearning to say less in, perhaps even leave, this unsafe space I naively thought was going to be safe, maybe even save me since I had stepped outside the box to become the first person in my family to pursue a PhD. The implications of her insult were clear: my Blackness, my queerness, unlocked the doors to NYU for me (maybe I checked those boxes on my application, maybe I didn't, but there was no room for the latter possibility in her mind). For that cohort mate, who I believe eventually became a tenure-track professor, I did not belong at NYU in the same way she did because, in her mind, merit unlocked the door for her. It couldn't have been her whiteness. She had to work to get to NYU, whereas my Blackness and my queerness simply worked the racist, homophobic system for me. Now, if any of that were possible, I would have my Blackness and queerness do a lot more for me than get me admitted to grad school, where I received a stipend that was less than half of the salary I made in the full-time Teach For America Connecticut Recruitment Director job I left behind to pursue the PhD (which turned out to be the right professional move for me, thankfully).

The lesson I began learning that day, a confusing lesson that took many years to internalize, was that an advanced degree does not make someone compassionate or pro-Black or a queer ally or even kind. The idea that all academics are smart, empathetic people devoid of bias, homophobia and racism, the kinds of toxic qualities one would assume they are educated about and understand in depth, was initially hard for me to accept. But just because someone is formally educated, and just because they are near me (forced academic, professional proximity), does not mean they care about me, like me or realize what it takes to be me in higher education. The unexpected contradictions were hard to reconcile, in part, because the deeper I stepped into academia, the more I began to see that my cohort mate was one of many white/non-Black people who think like her, a sobering reality.

In fact, I remember when I was an Assistant Professor a same-gender-loving white male colleague suggested something similar publicly on social media in 2019 about "diversity hires." I suppose he, too, thought I checked *all* the boxes. And I did: several innovative publications; an established, unique pedagogical methodology; and even some awards at that early point in my career. Yet, the point of his tweet was to reduce Black and queer scholars, or "diversity hires," to our identity markers that in his mind enabled us to take up white space, to take the places of white folks whose institutional degrees and elite pedigrees, not necessarily their achievements beyond earning the doctorate, somehow meant they deserved a magic carpet ride into the ivory tower's most coveted entry-level positions on the tenure track.

The experiences between grad school and my early tenure-track days were enough to begin shaping me into a same-gender-loving Black man who knows that contorting myself—my thinking, my body, my scholarship—for white comfort might be the death of me on some level. Shapeshifting and playing the respectability politics game was not going to save me as I played the tenure-track game. If anything, it was going to kill my spirit and stifle my long-term desire to cultivate a stable identity that would keep me in alignment, especially as it pertains to my mental health. Much like this chapter, and certainly because I came to realize my silence would not protect me, my scholarship and teaching are rooted in the authenticity of my same-gender-loving Black male self, a self that favors the tell-it-like-it-is pro-Black realness that keeps me from deluding myself into believing everyone in higher education wants me here. But, here I am. Here we same-gender-loving Black men are, despite the resistance, despite the sometimes energy-draining battles we fight on and off campus.

DOUBLE-PENETRATION, OR THE DUAL ASSAULT

The intersection of my Blackness and gayness complicates my experience in higher education, no doubt. The anti-Black racism *and* homophobia I can live through in any given moment, and have experienced, means the odds of being a target of hatred and ignorance are greater due to the odds of encountering someone who is racist or homophobic—or both. And when it is clearly both, that is when I, that is when we, experience the dual assault. As I reflect on my days on the 2014 academic job market, for instance, something that made my dream of advancing from grad student to college professor demoralizing was that the abysmal, very limited job market positions included institutions that would not deem me a good fit solely because I am queer, such as anti-gay religious schools. The job market list also included schools that would be incredibly hard for me to navigate even just on a personal level (in addition to the professional), such as institutions in places that have been historically hostile environments for BlaQueer people, making it explicitly clear how unwelcome we are in certain spaces.

Sometimes, the violence is more covert, but touching me nonetheless. Within the institutions I have worked at, I have found it necessary to try to adopt subtle strategies to protect my Black body, which happens to be muscular because I like exercise. At times, I have experienced colleagues, men and women, putting their hands on my body, on parts of my body that suggest the greeting is less about connecting and more about something they want to do to me in that moment. What that is specifically, I do not know. But I recall talking to a white woman colleague many years ago and, at one point, she put her hand on my thigh as she spoke to me while I was sitting on a highchair with my back to a wall. She was standing in front of me. Her hand remained on my thigh for an uncomfortably long time. As T. Anansi Wilson expresses with righteous rage, "White women sexually assault Black men every damn day and I'm tired as hell" (Wilson, 2017, para. 9). As a BlaQueer man, I sometimes find that women will touch me in ways they probably would not touch a heterosexual man because, for them, there is something unthreatening about physical contact with a man they think is not sexually attracted to them. But what about me? I should get to feel safe, too, in those moments when these women seemingly assume the role of heterosexual man with his hand on their thigh, a power move.

It should have been easy for me to request that this colleague simply remove her hand, but I was not sure how to do so diplomatically. And why did I think then that I had to be diplomatic, for it was *my* comfort and safety being sacrificed in that moment? Yet, there was no time for me to think. Rarely is there enough time for us to think and react to those unexpected uncomfortable situations. In a very Jordan Peele *Get Out* kind of way, I have experienced colleagues of both genders and various ages commenting on my physique, even touching or squeezing a body part, such as a bicep, as they greet me at a conference or on campus, my professional environments. I have wondered if my gay white male colleagues have similar experiences with being touched. But even if they do, does a touch or grab mean the same thing for their bodies as it does mine given the historical, and continued fetishization, of Black people's, Black men's, bodies (Foster, 2011)? Well, that's not really a serious question. In a world where Black people's bodies are constantly under attack, one would think folks, especially white folks, would be extra considerate about touch, about what the imbalanced racialized power dynamic means—or could mean.

Despite the challenges I have faced in higher education, and there are many (including issues I deal with in the classroom because of my identity and physicality), my BlaQueer professional life is not without great rewards that keep me invested in the vital work I do as a scholar, teacher and activist. The opportunity to use my BlaQueer life experience and philosophy to hopefully inspire people through my work is a privilege and joy I do not take for granted. I cannot take it for granted because the stakes are too high. Thus, in my scholarship, in my classroom and through public engagement, I do not exist to make people comfortable, for that would be a hypocritical goal or perhaps a betrayal of myself since I cannot be wholly comfortable unless I am in the safety of my own home or in a familiar, familial place I know is safe. As a BlaQueer man, I do not live in a world or exist in a society designed for my comfort. In truth, no one does, but there are levels to that discomfort. What I have come to appreciate about my positionality, as I assert at various moments in my book *Shakespeare's White Others* (Cambridge University Press), is that I get to pass on my "critical-personal-experiential" insights to my students and to people who engage seriously with me and my scholarship (Brown, 2023, 184).[3] Such opportunities are incredibly rewarding; they keep me striving in this profession.

Furthermore, my positionality as a same-gender-loving Black man has taught me to operate with a level of sensitivity and empathy that filters into how I interact with others, especially my students. Because I am pro-Black and openly gay, I get to serve as a living, accessible example for my students of someone who stands in authenticity. I get to show them how to use their voices and I do this, in part, by modeling for them how I use mine. Moreover, I get to encourage them to stand in the truth of who they are (and I show appreciation, I applaud them, when they do). I also get to inform my students about the costs of shrinking or losing themselves, of tolerating less than they deserve.

In my courses, the students are a captive audience. Therefore, it is my responsibility to use *their* time wisely so that maybe, just maybe, when they get to graduate school or to their first job they will respect the people around them, despite whatever differences may exist. And they will know how incredibly unprofessional and toxic it is to put other people down by projecting their own "perceived and felt inadequacy" onto others to build themselves up (Brown, 2021a, para 4).[4] It is my hope that my students will give everyone they encounter the utmost respect, just as they respect their peers in my classroom. I do not tolerate anything less in that environment. Having experienced anti-Black racism as far back in my life as I can remember, as early as around age five, and having experienced direct disrespect because I am gay, I have a wealth of reasons to actively activate activism in myself and others. When we use the negative to our advantage, we can transform the negative into a positive, thus allowing for redemption, maybe even catharsis, for the wounds we wear.[5]

SORRY, NOT SORRY

While it has taken me too many years to get to this place, I am certain now more than ever that my place in higher education must be one of meaningful disruption, especially for those who perpetuate the status quo. I can only achieve that goal, I

---

[3] For an illuminating look at *Shakespeare's White Others*, explore this interview conducted by Claudia Rankine: "David Sterling Brown," *Full Stop Magazine* (January 23, 2024): https://www.full-stop.net/2024/01/23/interviews/claudiarankine/david-sterling-brown/

[4] See Charlie Rose's interview with Toni Morrison: https://www.youtube.com/watch?v=5EQcy361vB8.

[5] On using the negative to one's advantage, I credit Dr. Milla Cozart Riggio for pushing my thinking on this front.

can only honor what I believe is my life's purpose, by showing up in authenticity. To bring my full self into higher education spaces means I am unapologetically me. It means I must not "come out" to people as gay, for example, but that I simply "let people in" to my world as they let me into theirs (Megarry, 2019, para. 3). It means I express myself unapologetically, as I have done here, about the difficulties and the rewards of moving through higher education as a BlaQueer man. Speaking of rewards: In August 2023, when Trinity College President Joanne Berger-Sweeney had me deliver the First-Year Convocation speech, I showed up exactly as I am—pink and orange, glitter-painted nails and all—so the students, and their parents and my own parents who were in the audience, could see me stand in authenticity at my alma mater and speak with integrity as I reflected on my academic and postgraduate journeys.[6] That professional opportunity was rewarding and enriching. It reaffirmed for me the value of not devaluing myself for the sake of other people's comfort.

To bring my full BlaQueer self into higher education spaces requires that in my work—scholarship, public-facing writing, presentations, collaborations, committees, Board memberships, pedagogy, all my work—I resist any desire not to act or not to have people hear my valid concerns or the valid concerns of my brothers and sisters. When we do that, we model what it means to be an "accomplice" who takes meaningful action as opposed to someone who merely thinks about taking action as the tragic hero *Hamlet* does for the majority of Shakespeare's famous play (Kendall, 2020, 257). In the end, Hamlet does kill his uncle Claudius, as he is instructed to do by his father's ghost, but there are costs for Hamlet's delay, as some Shakespeareans have argued (Peterson, 2021, 37). There are unnecessary human casualties over the course of that play as Hamlet thinks and thinks *and* thinks. I cannot afford to be like Hamlet, a figure some people, including my students, believe fails at his overall mission. Hamlet is a character whose success is debated by scholars who do not think he truly succeeds. It goes without saying that no one should aspire to be like Hamlet when there is vital work to be done.

"PRODUCTIVE DISCOMFORT" AND COMMUNITY CARE

As I close this chapter, it bears repeating that "life for me ain't been no crystal stair" (Hughes, 2002). And it is not lost on me that it will never be. I accept that. I cannot afford to resist that truth, no BlaQueer man should, for resistance is corrosive to the self. Resistance is distraction in a way that is akin to what the late, great Toni Morrison said about racism's function of being a distraction. And so, what exactly can higher education institutions do to support the brilliance that BlaQueer folk bring to the table? To start, institutions must be pro-Black advocates; they need to show unwavering support for the Black people in their spaces. In 2020, the world watched myriad Black Lives Matter protests and "anti-

---

[6] To hear the Convocation speech, which begins at the 53:20 timestamp, see https://www.youtube.com/watch?v=vUIYkTfQEfM

racist" movements unfold, some of which involved white and non-Black people, scholars included, performing advocacy and activism (and people still do this today). The 2020 faux activists even staged protest involvement for their social media posts, which they crafted only to help their so-called influencer statuses (Lankston, 2020). The performative gestures did nothing to help the true victims of anti-Black racism. Put simply, the influencers were incredibly uninfluential. Fast forward, and the world is still watching Black and queer folks get killed in the street, in the public realm (Brown & Little, 2021).[7] That leads me to ask a serious question: What good is anti-Black anti-racism? What good is it? And whom does it help? Not me or my Black mother, sister, or father and certainly not the late Jordan Neely or O'Shea Sibley .[8]

On that note, higher education institutions must acknowledge how dangerous the world's conditions are for BlaQueer folk, on and off college and university campuses. After acknowledging, I recommend they strategize concretely about how to help transform the conditions of the world. Do colleagues around the world ever consider, meditate on, what it means to be BlaQueer in a space that no doubt contains anti-Black and homophobic people who hide their disdain for my very existence? Probably not. Or at least not long enough to become so uncomfortable with injustice and inequity that they realize DEI is not the same as anti-racism and it is most definitely not the same as being pro-Black. As such, higher education institutions need to embrace meaningful rhetoric that derives from and simultaneously informs the actionable steps they can take to ensure the world becomes less dangerous for me, for my students, for my colleagues, for you and all who suffer because of anti-Black racism and homophobia. The gag is that everyone suffers, everyone—victims *and* perpetrators (Brown, 2021a).

Given that no one is exempt from suffering or being harmed in any given moment, I also recommend institutions eradicate "safe space" rhetoric because the question always remains: Safe for whom? When a young Black male rape victim sits in a classroom surrounded by peers who closely resemble his rapist, can he truly feel safe in that space? When I am the only BlaQueer person in my classroom, or when I am the sole BlaQueer person in a professional conference seminar room or Zoom session, is that a safe space for me given my countless past experiences with anti-Black racism? Rather than perpetuating the illusion of safety, I recommend higher education institutions embrace what I call "productive discomfort" in "(Early) Modern Literature: Crossing the 'Sonic Color Line'," for it is impossible, given the diverse lived experiences that people have, to ensure

---

[7] See "Invisible Bondage: The Other Side of Working on Shakespeare and Race in the Age of COVID19," Antiracism Series, Center for Literary and Comparative Studies, University of Maryland, September 2020 (featured speaker, with Arthur L. Little, Jr.) https://www.youtube.com/watch?v=OHTaNbkXrEk.

[8] See "O'Shea Sibley was killed after expressing queer joy, activists say." https://abcnews.go.com/US/oshea-sibley-killed-after-expressing-queer-joy-voguing/story?id=102129251. See "Subway Rider Choked Homeless Man to Death, Medical Examiner Rules." https://www.nytimes.com/2023/05/03/nyregion/nyc-subway-chokehold-death.html.

everyone feels safe in any given moment. Instead, higher education institutions should consider adopting radical, critically engaged practices that confront head-on the harsh realities of the real world to which they belong (Brown, 2021b, p. 56).[9] Pretending those realities do not exist in order to promote safe-space discourse, especially when the on- and off-campus life can never completely guarantee safety, serves no one in the short- or long-run, certainly not BlaQueer folk (Bouchrika, 2023).

Ultimately, I am convinced that retaining Black brilliance will be a continued challenge for higher education institutions so long as they do not recognize or honor how important safety—personal, physical, emotional, financial, intellectual, psychological safety—is for those of us who know our livelihoods are not our lives. We know this because we love ourselves enough to operate with healthy boundaries that remind us not to sacrifice any part of ourselves for our jobs. Dying on an institutional cross will not turn us into Jesus. Given this, I emphasize *loving* in my chapter's title because people must know that Black men, BlaQueer men, love and are capable of loving and being loved, a fact that pervasive anti-Black stereotypes work relentlessly to contradict. While it is true that the institution will not love us back, or love us Black, perhaps it should reconsider. A better, equitable future—my future, your future, our future—requires everyone to work toward generating and then manifesting revolutionary change in the world's higher education communities. Without such radical change, it will remain incredibly challenging for folks to operate in authenticity.

REFERENCES

Bouchrika, I. (2025). Coddling college students: Is the safe space movement working? *Research.com*. https://research.com/education/coddling-college-students

Brown, D. S. (2021a). *"Don't hurt yourself": (Anti)racism and white self-harm*. Los Angeles Review of Books. https://lareviewofbooks.org/article/antiracism-in-the-contemporary-university/ - _ftn2

Brown, D. S. (2021b). (Early) modern literature: Crossing the *"sonic* color line." In D. Henderson & K. Vitale (Eds.), *Shakespeare and digital pedagogy* (pp. 51–62). The Arden Shakespeare.

Brown, D. S. (2023). *Shakespeare's white others*. Cambridge University Press.

Brown, D. S., & Little, A. L. (November 2021). *To teach Shakespeare for survival: Talking with David Sterling Brown and Arthur L. Little*. Public Books. https://www.publicbooks.org/to-teach-shakespeare-for-survival-talking-with-david-sterling-brown-and-arthur-l-little-jr/

Carter, S. L. (1991). *Reflections of an affirmative action baby*. Basic Books.

Du Bois, W. E. B. (2011). *The souls of Black folk*. Tribeca Books.

Foster, T. A. (2011). The sexual abuse of Black men under slavery. *Journal of the History of Sexuality*, 20(3), 445–464. https://muse.jhu.edu/article/448992

hooks, b. (2015). *Black Looks: Race and Representation*. Routledge.

---

[9] For more on productive discomfort, see David Sterling Brown, "Discomfort Is the Point" in the American Association of University Professors magazine, *Academe* (February 2024).

Hughes, L. (1994). *The collected poems of Langston Hughes*. Knopf: Distributed by Random House.

Jones, D. M. (2005). *Race, Sex, and Suspicion: The myth of the Black male*. Greenwood Press.

Kendall, M. (2020). *Hood feminism: Notes from the women that a movement forgot*. Viking.

Lankston, C. (2020). "The whitest of white privilege": Influencers are blasted for using Black Lives Matter protests to gain "clout and followers" as videos of their "shameful" photo shoots in front of marches and looted stores are posted online. *The Daily Mail*. https://www.dailymail.co.uk/femail/article-8384259/Influencers-slammed-using-Black-Lives-Matter-protests-clout-followers.html

Lorde, A. (2017). *Your silence will not protect you*. Silver Press.

Megarry, D. (2019). Karamo Brown says we shouldn't use the phrase "coming out" anymore. *Gay Times*. https://www.gaytimes.co.uk/life/karamo-brown-says-we-shouldnt-use-the-phrase-coming-out-anymore

Peterson, K. L. (2021). *Hamlet*'s Touch of Picture. In S. Massai & L. Munro (Eds.), *Hamlet: The state of play* (pp. 27–50). The Arden Shakespeare.

Wiest, B. (2020). *The mountain is you: Transforming self-sabotage into self-mastery*. Thought Catalog Books.

Wilson, T. A. (2017). *We are not yours: I'm tired of white women's racial-sexual terrorism of my BlaQueer body*. Afropunk. https://afropunk.com/2017/11/not-im-tired-white-womens-racial-sexual-terrorism-blaqueer-body/

VIGNETTE FIVE

FITTING IN WHERE YOU GET IN!

Dr. D

It has been my experience as a Black gay male that working in higher education is an ideal environment. I attribute the conducive environment because of the vast amount of women who work in higher education. Higher education is predominantly occupied by women and makes it easier for a gay male to communicate, socialize in a work environment. The environment could be beneficial based off of the different age groups within The organization. I find it best when working with the older woman because they take on the motherly role, my peers share the same age because we can relate to the different times, and the younger women who are useful keeping me up-to-date with the changes in the world. I find it beneficial being in a safe space and avoiding drama associated at work. In addition, I find that communication is clearer in relationship building is stronger because of the natural bonds that occur. Depending on the maturity level, there can be great bonds associated with male coworkers And their understanding of gay culture. I've had the opportunity to meet great male, coworkers, and to bond in a different way without sexuality being at the forefront.

The Journey: Truths of Same-Gender-Loving Black Males in Higher Education, page 83.
Copyright © 2025 *Antione D. Tomlin*
Published under exclusive licence by Emerald Publishing Limited
ISBNs: 978-1-83708-498-2 HB, 978-1-83708-499-9 PB,
978-1-83708-500-2 EPDF, 978-1-83708-501-9 EPUB

NARRATIVE EIGHT

BARELY GETTING BI

Eric D. Martin

There are currently 107 historically Black colleges and universities (HBCUs) still open in the United States and of those, only four (4) have fully staffed LGBTQ centers. Leading the first center in the southeast region and the second oldest of the four campuses leaves room for a lot of other firsts, including being the first Black cis-male to serve as the coordinator of the center. While I knew accepting this role also meant accepting all the challenges that came with it, I was not prepared for the impact that this role would have on my own intersecting identities and the challenge of facing that impact. Suddenly, in addition to navigating a timeless battle of masculinity, I was also navigating the new feelings of bi-erasure in that same predominately Black space. In choosing to embark on this professional journey, the reality that I would be assumed gay was evident given the nature of the work, especially in higher ed, and was an identity I had no problem being assigned to. What I discovered to be the problem, however, was the general lack of bisexual representation in this field in tandem with my assimilation. This chapter will discuss the journey of learning to unpack this assimilation and its close relationship to the assimilation many Black men make to masculinity.

Keywords: Bisexuality, Black, Men, Higher Education, Queer, Same Gender Loving

The Journey: Truths of Same-Gender-Loving Black Males in Higher Education, pages 85–91.
Copyright © 2025 *Antione D. Tomlin*
Published under exclusive licence by Emerald Publishing Limited
ISBNs: 978-1-83708-498-2 HB, 978-1-83708-499-9 PB,
978-1-83708-500-2 EPDF, 978-1-83708-501-9 EPUB

BEING AN SGL IN HIGHER ED

Being an out professional in higher education is such a unique experience. For many of us, you are either embraced or ignored for the sake of HR compliance. In a world of new DEI 'efforts', it feels easier than it has in the past to just go along to get along. And for those of us who are embraced, it also means becoming the spokesperson for our intersecting identities. Suddenly, now that a same-gender-loving (SGL) man is on staff, more conversations about inclusivity start being brought to the table, or in my case, an interest in collaboration that can sometimes feel like pacified representation rather than inclusion. Being an SGL man in higher education means being aware of all of this. It means choosing your battles and protecting your peace. This incredibly complex and nuanced identity means that I have to constantly be prepared to engage with those individuals who have had the privilege of being an average child who grew into an average adult. Individuals who had the luxury of not questioning their existence, thriving in a cisgender-heterosexual world without even a hint of fear of any kind of violence or abandonment. For me as a professional involved in student engagement being an out, Black SGL man means finding my footing and remembering that many of the professionals I come across will never understand what it is to be me in my fullness. As humans, we all come with unique things about us, identities that are constantly fluctuating with the ebbs and flows of power and privilege, and for that, I have grace and empathy. However, there is something about being a Black SGL man in higher education that only those who share this specific identity will understand and it makes building community that much more of a necessity.

MY EXPERIENCE AS AN SGL IN HIGHER ED

By day, I serve as a DEI professional at a historically Black university (HBCU) who trains, supervises, and spearheads programming for the LGBTQ+ community on campus while leading an LGBTQ+ center. It's something that I am incredibly proud of, considering that my campus is only one of four HBCUs to have a fully staffed center out of 107 institutions. We are among the small but mighty and I am grateful to be one of the few higher education professionals dedicated to doing the work of inclusion and equity for our students. But I would be remiss if I failed to discuss just how nuanced my role is concerning this institution type, the culture that comes with it, and most importantly, my own intersecting identities; all of which shape and inform how I navigate this field.

Being an out higher ed professional is a tricky experience to navigate. Typically, you fall into one of two categories: the DEI spokesperson, or the troublemaker with intent on spreading the infamous gay agenda. I've had the pleasure and the misfortune of being both. As a queer professional, the role and responsibility of representation are bestowed upon you whether you want it or not. And in a space where shared identities, all at the intersection of Blackness, exist simultaneously, conflict is almost inevitable. And given the nature of my work and job title, I am, in many ways, expected to be the troublemaker in the room when the truth is that challenging masculinity can be incredibly difficult.

Any space that tends to lean heavily into straightness can easily become a place where inappropriate comments and opinions surrounding misogyny and homophobia often go unchecked, largely because of the camaraderie. Across the room, there is a sense of sameness that unites participants, dismissing the idea that anyone in this sacred space may have a difference in opinion. One program in particular that I attended, hosted by the men's center at my institution called for us all to be in community to discuss some matters of life. An evening no different than I would host, a space where students and staff can get together and unpack some of the popular culture that was impacting student life; this evening being the topic of gender roles. As one can probably imagine, in a space where unconscious biases often run rampant, some things were said that left me with a large feeling of disagreement. When I entered that space, ready to offer a bit of challenge to the discussion, it disrupted not only the flow, but immediately damaged the unspoken vow of trust that everyone, including myself, was expected to follow upon entering. Suddenly with that swift moment of disagreement, the feeling of betrayal washed over the room, and I felt the disconnect. It's a feeling I know too well to take personally but does not make it any less frustrating. The level of unlearning that I want for my students and colleagues is something that I cannot want for them or force them into. However, harmful behavior is something I also cannot tolerate. This constant dichotomy of my salient identities is something that I, as an SGL professional, have to leverage daily while staying mindful of how I choose to continue to show up for myself and my identities.

I would be lying if I said that being in that space was not a triggering experience. Even while standing on my adult principles and beliefs, it is challenging to witness students avoid me and my center out of fear of being associated with what my center offers and the students who frequent the space. As a queer man, that feeling of not being wanted by your own is a way too familiar feeling that for many of us, still triggers a fight or flight feeling of assimilation. This incident happened early in this role and forced me to take inventory of how I wanted to show up daily. Given the nature of the work, I knew that I would be assumed gay by the majority of people that I worked with, and it was something that I didn't mind in the beginning. Because I knew queerness was so expansive, I didn't feel the need to correct people when they made those kinds of assumptions. However, after attempting to extend an olive branch to some of the men on campus, I pondered if naming my bisexuality and my opposite-sex attractions would allow me in spaces with other people to take me more seriously as a professional. What I was learning from this institution was that relationships were not the only important part of getting what you needed, but it was also about the level of comfortability and relatability. If you could be related to, you had the power in the interaction. I considered what it would be like to be more passing to Black male students that I wanted to reach. Should I deepen my tone of voice? Do I go for the handshake or fist pound rather than a hug? All questions I muddled over for the sake of making them comfortable. I knew that they would likely never come to me, so what would it look like to come to them? What would it look like to try and meet them on their level to educate from the inside out? Could I still plant the seeds I wanted to plant without triggering that feeling of betrayal from both parties? Choosing to think differently from my in-group members meant committing myself to being 'different'. It also meant that in most instances, I was no longer relatable and therefore, not worth investing in socially. For the larger part of my first few months I battled with this approach, trying to figure out the best course of action that made sense for me. What I realized, however, was that this feeling of assimilation that I was feeling, this need to avoid that feeling of betrayal from students and colleagues was unsustainable.

In the months after this event, I spent some long days and nights finishing up my grad program. As a part of those requirements, I chose to emphasize my capstone on unpacking masculinity among Black men. This meant another attempt to develop professional relationships with students and staff of the center. What I was not prepared for, however, was the level of participation that I was to receive from students and the level of depth and variety in the conversation that was paired with it. In the end, I was able to interview six individuals, all of whom shared unique and vulnerable parts of themselves with me. Through these 30-minute interviews, I was able to discover just how multifaceted these young men were, regardless of their identities. I asked about their learned sense of masculinity, belongingness, and their interpersonal relationships. I discovered that some were poets, theater majors, musicians, or all-around R&B lovers all on their personal journeys with masculinity. Some were more traditional, while others were like me, using the space to be disruptors to the harmful behavior. It was an eye-opening experience to hear firsthand from these men that there was more to them than their presentation. And continues to shape my practice today. For us both, in what felt like a first in a while, assimilation was not on the table. I was no longer trying to fit into their, my straight students, world, and they did not need to shy away from mine. Both parties didn't feel the need to put on the mask of passing for the sake of being comfortable. And in those brief moments, that feeling of erasure of my queerness that I was used to feeling simply didn't exist.

Given the nature of my work, identity is a prominent factor in not only my role as an administrator but who I am as a Black, queer man. I have to constantly remind myself that I deserve the same amount of grace that I give my students when it comes to figuring out what works for me. Belongingness is not something that is reserved for the traditional college-aged student. It is a value that all professionals should have an understanding of that hopefully makes them comfortable in their roles.

CHALLENGES & REWARDS

As a queer Black man, I am no stranger to marginalization. It is a part of my identity that I carry with me no matter where I go, work being no different. While I have been incredibly fortunate to be on a campus that is home to a variety of centers where students can have their needs met outside the classroom, my biggest reward is also my biggest challenge. Being a physical manifestation and representation of a queer Black male professional means coming up against the infamous experience of masculinity and its relation to the ever-so-silent battle of maleness vs. queerness

The best word that I can use to describe the feelings that radiate from my cisgender-heterosexual counterparts is betrayal. If ever I have challenged the thought process of another Black man at work, encouraging him to think beyond the traditional confines of gender and sexual orientation, the reaction is the same; defensiveness and dismissal. Causing an eruption of opinions in a room full of people, including colleagues and students, all surprised that we do not all think the same way is always an interesting experience that brings up frustration on both ends stemming from the same question of 'How could you?' Choosing to stand in my queerness and be a vocal representation in the room is a challenge that I never back down from. It is with the understanding that queerness for many men and male-identified students is a silent battle and assimilation often feels like the only way to win. Being an SGL professional challenges me and encourages me to continuously examine my place within my communities and take inventory of what experiences I know to be true and those I want to unlearn. Masculinity is a framework that takes hold of two salient parts of my identity that I actively work against both personally and professionally because the reality is my lived experience cannot be separated. The biggest challenge and reward that no one prepared me for when I became an out professional is the level of responsibility that comes with representation.

BRINGING MY FULL AUTHENTIC SELF

I've spent a lot of my life not taking up space and making myself small in both physical and metaphorical ways. As a man of size, in addition to my queerness, taking the space I deserve has always been a challenge for me, which left room for folks to tell my story based on how they perceived me. For many years there was a deafening silence that I lived my life by, operating in a space of "that's fine" for the sake of keeping the peace. I convinced myself that I had to keep the nuances of my invisible identity to myself and assimilate into the world around me instead of creating a world of my own, even professionally. What I am just now learning, however, is that none of the latter is true.

Being my full and authentic self in higher education spaces means knowing and believing that I deserve to be in these professional spaces. Understanding that the hard work that I've put in, in both my personal and professional lives has led me here and is more than enough. My academic journey is enough, my experience is enough, and my personal story is enough because I am enough. It means learning to trust my process, being more vocal about the amazing intersectional journey that I will be on for the rest of my life, and inviting the people I trust on that journey. In many ways, I have allowed myself to suffer in silence, thinking that because part of my identity was invisible, I was also invisible and that is not the case. Showing up as myself means taking up the space that I not only deserve but that the people around me who love and care about me also want me to have. Showing up for myself means silencing the voice of imposter syndrome that says I can't and giving the energy to the voice that says you can and you will. Bringing myself also means healing and refusing to carry baggage that is not my own. I have allowed other people to take up space in my world, causing me to neglect myself and the things I love. Thankfully, through therapy and connecting with my inner child, I can recognize that the only person in control of the life that I want to live and the person I am to become is me. This includes all parts of me, Blackness and queerness alike.

As a queer Black person in America, the odds have been stacked against me since birth. However, what I am learning in this season of my life is that putting down other people's baggage is just as important as taking inventory of my own. I cannot and will not continue to operate in a space of letting other people tell my story based on how they *think* they know me. Showing up in my authentic Blackness and queerness means allowing people to see me in ways that I used to be afraid to show, using my voice to give breath to the invisible parts of my identity, and naming the fact that all parts of me stand proudly in this room. This role, my place in higher education continues to teach me that healing is a journey and not a destination. It is ongoing and the more I show up for myself, the more space I take up, the more I tame negative self-talk and stir clear of assimilation, and the more whole, confident, and present I become. In this work, you are only as good as you feel on the inside and my soul deserves peace and my mind deserves ease. Walking in my truth as a higher education professional who knows his worth and will settle for *nothing* less will get me that.

TIPS & RECOMMENDATIONS

And in a perfect world, I wouldn't have to settle. I would be at an institution that understands that intersectionality is not solely a framework that applies to students, but to faculty and staff members as well. There would be a sense of advocacy on behalf of the identities, both visible and invisible, that don't always make it into the room. An institution that understands its role in an oppressive history and hires staff members who actively work against that history are major stakeholders in this game of equity. Shying away from the exclusive history of higher education does nothing for anyone, especially the Black and brown staff that work for these institutions. No decisions can be made for us, without us. Meaning we need to be at the table and if we aren't there needs to be someone at the table using their privilege to fight for our ability to gain access to the table. I'm sure many SGL men share similar sentiments as I, those who allow themselves to feel small, but in many ways, it's not solely our job to make ourselves feel big. To take up space, there has to be space to take. Acknowledging the brilliance and the power that true diversity, equity, and inclusion have creates space for representation, community building, and empowerment in ways that can enrich all of higher education. This looks like understanding the cultural and societal differences that come along with each intersecting identity. This looks like allowing Black professionals the space to be themselves in their gender expression with our dress and hair, within our speech, and our communal spaces.

The reality is that two of the identities I'm most proud of have been under attack the most, and as per usual, I am expected to keep my head up and push through. So, while my resiliency may be the key to my success, working in a field at an institution that values all the brilliance that I bring is also key. And that kind of valuing begins with myself. It means unlearning all the negative self-talk, behaviors, and internalized oppression that I have exhibited over myself. Systemic racism is not my baggage to hold, nor is homophobia. Unlearning the ways that I have hindered myself allows me to be bold in my identity and shape the experience that I want from the place(s) I work. And institutions of higher education, regardless of type, should understand that the wave of unlearning that is happening among professionals does not mean stagnation. This is a train already in motion and has been for several hundred years. Gone are the days of complacency and willful ignorance. It is my recommendation that institutions surrender the idea of seeing if I'm a good fit for them and embrace the fact that they may not be a good fit for me. I've spent a lot of time, too much if I'm honest in a place of professional uncertainty. But I'm here now. Finally understanding what I need to do to get **Bi**.

BIOGRAPHIES

EDITOR'S BIO

Antione D. Tomlin, Ph.D. Rooted in core values like Autonomy, Flexibility, Learning, Respect, Transparency, Honesty, and Fun, I live and breathe principles that not only shape my life but also guide my interactions with others. As a proud native of Baltimore City, these values have been my compass in navigating life's journey. Being a first-generation undergrad and grad student, I recognize the transformative power of education, a value intricately tied to my passion for continuous learning. This passion steered me into a fulfilling career in higher education, where I've been teaching English since 2013. The classroom, for me, is an ever-inspiring space filled with dedicated students who continually fuel my curiosity and growth. Beyond teaching, I wear the hat of a trained and certified Life and Engagement Coach, proudly holding the Professional Certified Coach (PCC) credential from the International Coach Federation (ICF). Feel free to explore more about my coaching venture, Best AT Coaching!, LLC. As a Baltimore native, I earned my academic stripes from local institutions: a BS in psychology from Stevenson University, an MA in higher education administration and student affairs from Morgan State University, and a PhD in language, literacy, and culture

The Journey: Truths of Same-Gender-Loving Black Males in Higher Education, pages 93–97.
Copyright © 2025 *Antione D. Tomlin*
Published under exclusive licence by Emerald Publishing Limited
ISBNs: 978-1-83708-498-2 HB, 978-1-83708-499-9 PB,
978-1-83708-500-2 EPDF, 978-1-83708-501-9 EPUB

from the University of Maryland, Baltimore County. My current research focuses on the experiences of Black and Brown faculty, staff, and students in higher education. For more about Antione visit drantionetomlin.com

AUTHOR BIOS

David Sterling Brown is an award-winning, tenured Associate Professor of English at Trinity College (Connecticut). He is the author of *Shakespeare's White Others* (Cambridge University Press), which was acquired by Tantor Media and recorded as an audiobook, with Brown as narrator. He has published numerous peer-reviewed and public-facing essays and delivered myriad talks. He is also an editor and public speaker. In 2021, he received a prestigious Mellon/ACLS Scholars and Society Fellowship that facilitated his residency with Claudia Rankine's The Racial Imaginary Institute, of which he is a full-time Curatorial Team member. The Fellowship also facilitated the development of his professional website (www.DavidSterling-Brown.com) and his virtual-reality art gallery and exhibition—"Visualizing Race Virtually"—that complements *Shakespeare's White Others*. His second book, *Hood Pedagogy*, will be published by Cambridge University Press. In the meantime, he is working on a few articles for different scholarly venues.

Andrew B. Campbell (DR.ABC) is an Assistant Professor, Teaching Stream in Leadership for Racial Justice in Education, and the Teaching and Learning Coordinator for the Master of Teaching program at the University of Toronto. DR.ABC is well known to the OISE community for his leadership on advancing anti-discrimination work in teacher education and received OISE's 2022 award for Excellence in Initial Teacher Education. He presently teaches courses in anti-discrimination education, leadership and diversity, educational change, urban education, and Black Educators pedagogy and practice. He has presented at numerous conferences and has delivered many presentations as a keynote speaker, motivational speaker, and workshop facilitator. He loves people, food, fashion, traveling and bringing his community together for a good meal.

Anthony Davis is from the thriving city of Baltimore Maryland. He earned a Bachelor's Degree from Stevenson University, majoring in Film. He also enjoys cooking, watching sports and creating memories with his friends and family.

Desmond Dunklin currently serves as the Interim Associate Director of University Programs at the University of South Alabama. He holds a Bachelor's Degree in Early Childhood Education, a Master's Degree in Higher Education, and is currently pursuing his PhD. in Higher Education Administration. An advocate for African American Males in higher Education, Desmond spends his time mentoring, coaching and working with various associations to increase the awareness of African American Males students' success for Black Males attending Predominantly White Institutions (PWIs).

Andre' Ford is currently a candidate for a Doctor of Social Work degree in Organizational Leadership at the University of Alabama. He completed his Bachelor of Arts degree in History, Theater Arts and Secondary Teaching Education from Saint Edward's University. Since 2005, he has worked in both non for profit and in higher education in New York City, as a teacher, adjunct lecturer and program manager of adult continuing education and vocational training programs. In 2014, he received his Master of Social Work degree, with a concentration in Organizational Management and Leadership, with a specialization in Children, Youth and Families from Hunter College. His research interests include: how to make programs, institutions, and organizations that serve LGBTQIA+ Black, Indigenous and people of color more inclusive and identity affirming, the successful retention and graduation of African American males in the continuum of social work education, the intersectionality of authentic spirituality and social work practice, and the development of a community-based holistic care model for Gay and Bisexual+ African American men who are transitioning from young to middle age adulthood.

Aaron Hargrove, PharmD, with a passion for healthcare and extensive research experience, I have gained expertise in various therapeutic areas. My areas of expertise include drug discovery and development, clinical trials, and regulatory affairs. Through my academic journey, I have published numerous research papers and presented my work at prestigious conferences. I am committed to advancing scientific knowledge and improving patient outcomes through evidence-based practices. With strong communication skills and a collaborative mindset, I thrive in interdisciplinary environments. My diversity as a black gay scientist brings a unique perspective to my work, enabling me to address health disparities and advocate for marginalized communities. Overall, I am dedicated to making a positive impact on the field of pharmacy and advancing the well-being of individuals through research and innovation.

Rodrick C. Johnson is a dynamic literacy coach, educator, and CEO of Energized Educator, dedicated to empowering teachers and transforming classrooms. With a visionary approach, Rodrick nurtures educators to unlock their full potential, fostering a culture of excellence and innovation in education. Through his leadership, he inspires teachers to embrace data-informed instruction, guiding them on a journey from proficiency to mastery. As a Great Minds Fellow, Rodrick has impacted hundreds of educators nationwide, championing professional development and curriculum enhancements. With a background in crafting enriching learning environments and a commitment to reshaping teacher preparation, he pursues a doctorate at Morgan State University, aiming to drive positive change in education policy and practice. Rodrick's passion for empowering educators and fostering student success underscores his mission to revolutionize teaching and learning for generations to come.

Brandon Mack is the founder/owner of B.Mack Strategies, a full service consulting firm dedicated to building unapologetic equity through college admissions/access, education, training, and facilitation. He is a former Associate Director of Admission at Rice University and former Interim Director of Operations at the International Association for College Admissions Counseling. He has been an activist/organizer/angelic troublemaker focusing on the intersections of racial justice, LGBTQ+ issues, and education for over 20 years.

Richard Marks, Jr, hailing from Indianapolis, IN, currently serves as the Assistant Vice President for Diversity and Innovative Community Engagement and holds the position of Executive Director of the Cross-Cultural for Global Citizenship at Saint Louis University. He is an alum of Indiana University, Bloomington, where he earned his Bachelors in African American Studies/Sociology and a Masters in Higher Education Administration in Student Affairs. He obtained his doctorate in Educational Leadership from the Rossier School of Education at the University of Southern California. Dr. Marks' doctoral dissertation, titled "As the World Turns: Being Black and Gay on Campus in the 21st Century," delves into the experiences of Black gay men at a predominantly White institution (PWI) in southern California. His research explores the intricate intersections of race, sexual identity, and social capital-institutional agents, revealing themes such as self-identity, coming-out, racial & cultural dissonance, (toxic) masculinity, religion/spirituality, institutional support, and family affairs. With over two decades of experience in higher education, His extensive expertise is evident in his facilitation and presentations covering various topics such as race in higher education, LGBTQ issues, toxic masculinity, gender roles and expressions, Greek life, diversity training, team building, leadership, intersectionality, and identity

Eric Martin, M.S. is a speaker and educator, centered on the advancement of marginalized communities of color in higher education. Currently situated at Columbia University, Martin leads community development, and student leadership training, and maintains chief oversight as the Program Director of LGBTQ@Columbia. Dedicated to the betterment and inclusion of Black and queer students within the higher education space, Eric facilitates specific and intentional programs that challenge and empower students, faculty, and staff to become more inclusive and understand intersecting identities. Beyond the institution, Eric is a member of the Pan-African Network through the American College Personnel Association (ACPA). Eric holds two bachelor's degrees, one in English, the other in psychology, and a master's degree in higher education from North Carolina Central University (NCCU). He currently lives in Brooklyn.

Sean Rice, Jr., M.S., originally from Portland, Oregon, began fostering his talents in leadership and creative spaces at a young age. By high school, he led his peers as Senior Class President and received a full-ride scholarship that took him to Memphis, TN. While pursuing his Advertising degree, he balanced two jobs with maintaining his honors status. Unable to find employment in advertising, he moved up the ranks of the hospitality industry but wanted to make an impact. Sean then returned to school to earn his Master's in Student Affairs, focusing on conflict resolution and analysis. After exploring opportunities in other areas, he invested his talents and training in the student support and case management functional area which he currently does in his role as the Assistant Director of Triage and Case Coordination at Brown University. Outside of work, Sean enjoys curating spaces to celebrate both his Blackness and Queerness.

Kelly Wallace is a native of Prince George's County Maryland. He obtained his doctorate in Couples & Family Therapy from Drexel University. He holds a Master of Arts in Clinical Mental Health Counseling from The Chicago School of Professional Psychology and a bachelor's degree in psychology from Bowie State University. He also holds a Postgraduate Certificate from Northcentral University in Family Therapy. Dr. Kelly Wallace is a Couple/Marriage & Family Therapist and a Professional Counselor. In therapy, he utilizes a systemic/integrative approach which allows for a unique design to treatment for clients and helps individuals, couples and families recognize historical, cultural, and social influence on their physical, emotional, spiritual, social, sexual and professional selves.

He is also a professor and teaches in couples and family therapy, clinical mental health counseling, and human services programs. He is also a mentor to future clinicians. He also uses his skills as a learning and development consultant to various private practices, institutions, and other organizations dedicated to mental wellness, advocacy and social justice of misrepresented and underrepresented communities. He has presented at state and national conferences. He also shares his expertise on blogs and articles, promoting mental health wellness.

Kaschka R. Watson, PhD (He/Him), is a Jamaican-born Canadian scholar. He is an Assistant Professor of Administration, Leadership, and Policy in the Faculty of Education in the Department of Educational Studies at Brock University. His teaching, research, and advocacy reflect his passion for championing initiatives that identify, disrupt, and dismantle inequities in education for marginalized students. He is recognized as a change-maker and transformative leader in the field. Dr. Watson's scholarly work in social justice has fostered equitable opportunities for schools, racialized students, educational leaders, institutions, and stakeholders. His research interests are informed by anti-racism, administration, leadership, policy, diversity, inclusion, equity, and social justice themes in Canadian schools and universities. His academic contributions include journal reviews, book chapters, and magazine articles. In addition to his scholarship, his advocacy and activism have produced several publications that challenge Canadian education systems and institutions to develop more equitable environments for racialized students at K-12, college, and university levels.